JETHART'S HERE!

JETHART'S HERE!

The GARY ARMSTRONG Story

Gary Armstrong AND Derek Douglas

FOREWORD BY Bill McLaren

MAINSTREAM
PUBLISHING
EDINBURGH AND LONDON

First published in Great Britain in 1995 by
MAINSTREAM PUBLISHING COMPANY (EDINBURGH) LTD
7 Albany Street
Edinburgh EH1 3UG

ISBN 1 85158 727 6

A catalogue record for this book is available from the British Library

Typeset in Garamond by Litho Link Ltd, Welshpool, Powys, Wales
Printed and bound in Great Britain by Butler & Tanner Ltd, Frome

CONTENTS

PHOTOGRAPHIC ACKNOWLEDGMENT

THE AUTHORS are grateful to *The Herald* newspaper for permission to reproduce many of the photographs which appear in *Jethart's Here!*

FOREWORD

By Bill McLaren, OBE

IT MAY have come as something of a surprise to his many friends and admirers that the inimitable Gary Armstrong has agreed to put his story into print for he always has been the most modest and self-effacing of men, not given to using five words if two would do and, through his marvellous career, more inclined to let his play do his talking for him.

This, however, is a story worth telling about one of the truly great Rugby Union players of our time who, despite the fame thrust upon him, has kept his feet firmly on the ground, has always called it as he has seen it, and never purported to be anything other than the person he is, an uncomplicated fellow with simple tastes and a clear picture of what he hopes life would have to offer him.

Nor has he ever deviated from the set of values that he has deemed essential to the integrity of life and, amid all the adulation heaped upon him for his splendid feats on the rugby field and his strong character off it, he has treated it all with that distinctive, laid-back attitude that is an Armstrong hallmark whilst also showing unswerving loyalty to family, friends and to club, town and country.

That family loyalty runs deep, a matter brought forcibly to my attention by a forthright lady of Gary's close acquaintance, his grandmother, Betty Paxton. During one match commentary I made the point that Gary's 'shilpeet' look hardly created the impression of rude physical strength. Sometimes, one ventured to suggest, Gary looked as if he could do with a right good meal. Not so long afterwards I was upbraided in front of the entire Hawick club stand for daring to infer that Gary did not enjoy the very best of feeding. Betty certainly put me in my place!

In fact Gary has been one of the strongest scrum-halves ever to wear the number 9 jersey, one who has vied with forwards in ball winning and protection and retention and whose force of tackle has been quite shattering. I still can see the pained expression on the face of that rugged English back-row forward, Mike Teague, when he was in full flight from his own scrummage pick-up at Murrayfield in 1990, and was almost cut in half by the blistering force of the Armstrong engagement.

New Zealanders never offer praise lightly. Their respect has to be hard earned. It was therefore an indication of Gary Armstrong's standing in the world game that, during Scotland's tour there in 1990, hard-bitten New Zealanders heaped praise on him as one of the best they ever had seen. Coming in a country renowned for producing scrum-halves out of the top drawer, that was some accolade.

It is small wonder that stand-off halves revel in playing with Gary for he runs a partner protection society in which he is the only shareholder! One cannot recall an occasion when he handed on rubbish ball to his partner. In that riveting Grand Slam decider at Murrayfield in 1990 when England were on the ascendant Gary received lineout ball that had 'Ward 10' written all over it. He realised that a pass would render his team-mate a sitting duck to a destruction-intent Peter Winterbottom, didn't go through with the pass but, instead, took heavy flak himself from England's forwards.

Another distinctive aspect of his play that often catches opponents by surprise and frequently leaves them clutching fresh air is his ability to run at pace in a low, jack-knife position. He not only has been able to beat opponents with sidestep, swerve, lethal hand-off and change of pace but underneath them as well!

This is a story of many highs and some lows, of accepting the rough with the smooth, of high success as a British Lion in 1989 and a key member of Scotland's Grand Slam squad of 1990, of 30 Scottish caps, 26 as half-back partner to Craig Chalmers thus continuing a recent Border tradition as successors to that other ham and eggs combination, John Rutherford and Roy Laidlaw. It is a story also about frustration and disappointment as serious knee damage threatened to end a famous career, about strength of character, patience and dogged resolve in taking on the painful task of injury recovery, of, as one example, dragging heavy weights up and down Riverside Park like a dray horse as part of that task under the watchful gaze of his friend and taskmaster, Brian 'Chico' Woods.

It never was going to be an easy task to select Gary Armstrong's greatest moment. He had so many of them! Yet two internationals, in my view, bore a special Armstrong stamp — the Grand Slam decider with England at Murrayfield in 1990 and Scotland's World Cup quarter-final win over Ireland at Murrayfield in 1991. In the former he made a typical and crucial contribution to the Tony Stanger try that virtually won the Slam. It was a wee touch of Armstrong magic in cheekiness, timing and technique that tended to be taken for granted amid the euphoria of a famous score. Remember how John Jeffrey fed Gary from a scrummage pick-up and Gavin Hastings placed a pin-point punt for Stanger to use his 6ft 2in to reach high to gather and dot down? Yet it was the momentary threat by Gary Armstrong that checked Teague and Rob Andrew prior to that delicately threaded Armstrong pass that opened the way for Hastings.

Gary also has the gift for creating among opposing scrum-halves the impression of being an animated octopus around the fringes. It was when England were throwing the kitchen sink at Scotland in the closing minutes of that Slam decider that England won superbly channelled scrummage ball. Yet with perfect timing, and a mid-air launch that would have done credit to an

Olympic swimmer off his pad, Gary completely wrecked Richard Hill's pick-up and even managed to leap to his feet in time to receive the ball from Finlay Calder before improvising a punt through the eye of a needle for a safe touch and a welcome respite.

The World Cup quarter-final against Ireland was precariously balanced when Gary Armstrong more or less took the game by the throat to inspire Scotland's 24–15 win. Having lost through injury his regular partner, Craig Chalmers, Gary then took on much of the responsibility for the tactical direction, thus easing the pressure on replacement stand-off Graham Shiel who, partly as a result, had a splendid match. There was another masterly demonstration of Gary Armstrong's variety of punt placement, notably his gift for clearing messy ball with lateral and even backwards drift before angling the punt over his left shoulder. There was also a mazy run through cluttered confines and with pugnacity written all over it by which he set confident Irishmen back on their heels. The coup de grâce was administered by the Riverside Park middleweight when he ignited Shiel, then looped him, for the clinching try.

It was true to character that whether he was playing for Jed-Forest, the South, Scotland 'B', for whom he scored three tries on his début, the Barbarians, the national side or the Lions, Gary Armstrong always has given 100 per cent, has placed his body on the line and, in his own quiet way, sought to inspire colleagues into similar deeds of derring-do.

Gary Armstrong's impact upon the Rugby Union game as player and character has earned him the highest esteem from friend and foe alike and not least for his simple philosophy that there are some things more important than fame and money such as wife Shona, children, Darren and Nicole, and family and genuine friends.

His importance to the Scottish cause can hardly be overemphasised. Why otherwise would the Scottish Rugby Union and his employers have been so keen to create special circumstances that might hasten his return to the fray? Hopefully there is still a fair measure of petrol in his tank and that he will grace the thistled jersey again.

Meanwhile, he and Derek Douglas have combined to produce a thoroughly enjoyable story that surely will give immense pleasure as a popular addition to the literature of the great game. After all, it is about a genuine class act.

Bill McLaren,
Hawick

CHAPTER 1

MIDDLE GREEN TO MURRAYFIELD

The Journey Begins Here

PEEL HOSPITAL, an interconnected village of wooden-hutted wards which stood in the countryside near Galashiels, was a grim place at the best of times. It's gone now, replaced by a brand, spanking new Borders General Hospital at Tweedbank between Melrose and Galashiels. But to a bewildered six-year-old with an excruciating pain in his right leg, this scattered collection of wooden huts built during World War II looked like the end of the earth.

It was the winter of 1972. It seemed to me that at one moment I had been a happy-go-lucky youngster getting up to all of the mischief that happy-go-lucky youngsters get up to. And then the next I was confined to bed at Peel Hospital and separated from the family and friends who meant so much to me then and who have continued to play a central role in my life ever since.

The doctor's diagnosis had come as a tremendous shock to my dad, Lawrence, and mum, Margaret. So far as I was concerned I couldn't even pronounce what the doctor had said was wrong with me. All I knew that it was a big word and it was bloody sore! I had osteomyelitis.

To this day my dad suffers pangs of guilt whenever the word is mentioned. I've never been much of a one to sing the praises of school life. No doubt school suited some folk but as a six-year-old I looked upon it as something which had to be tolerated but which got in the way of the really important things in life. Put it another way, I was forever on the lookout for reasons and excuses which would mean that I wouldn't have to drag myself into school.

On this particular weekend we were out at The Pinnacle, near Jedburgh, where my grandfather was the farm steward. The outdoor life was the one for me and whenever I was out on the farm everything was well with the world. We were sawing logs when I first felt the pain in my right ankle. I put up with it for a wee while in silence and then it started to become really sore. When I told Dad he just gave me one of those old-fashioned looks. He had heard me prattling on before about this ache and that pain. And it was funny that they always seemed to arise on a Sunday when the dreaded prospect of school loomed the next day.

Well, it was a Sunday and I had another ache to report. Only this time it was true. I sat on a tree trunk and put my case to Dad. I had a really bad pain in my ankle and I felt really rotten. Dad took a look and couldn't see anything amiss. As the afternoon and evening wore on the pain didn't get any better. By now Mum and Dad were convinced that I was putting on a performance of Oscar-winning proportions. When bedtime came around I was still complaining that my leg was sore and that I couldn't go to school next day. Dad gave me a skelp around the lug and told me to get off to bed. They would see how I felt the next day.

Mum and Dad obviously thought that they had seen off my efforts to skip school and that next morning I would be back to my cheery self. When Monday came, though, the pain was no better. In fact it was worse.

My parents were now extremely concerned that there was, indeed, something far amiss and that on this occasion I hadn't been 'crying wolf'. Dad rushed me down to see our GP who declared that I wasn't at all well and that I should be admitted to hospital right away. I was whipped off to Peel Hospital where the diagnosis of osteomyelitis was confirmed. Apparently it is an inflammation of the bone marrow caused by an infection and in those days it was pretty serious. Maybe it still is.

Dad went back home to Jedburgh with my clothes in a paper bag. When Mum saw what he had under his arm she was grief-stricken. My parents couldn't believe how quickly the thing had struck and they couldn't forgive themselves for just dismissing it as another of my 'get out of school' ploys.

I couldn't believe it myself. It seemed like a nightmare. But it was real enough and I was to spend the next two months away from my family as a result. I don't know what the situation is now but when I was struck by the disease there were a number of alternative treatments and, by luck or good judgment, the one that the medics tried first was the one that most suited me. Nevertheless, I spent eight weeks immobile in bed with my leg in plaster. As you might imagine, for a 'perpetual motion' kid like I was as a six-year-old, the prospect of spending eight hours in bed, never mind eight weeks, was something which didn't really bear thinking about. And for that matter it doesn't really bear thinking about right now!

Over the next eight weeks my family and friends made the 40-mile round trip to visit me on an almost daily basis. But the dark memory of those days still haunts me and, maybe, is responsible for the firm grip which my home town still has on me. Like many small towns, Jedburgh — which stands just miles from the English border — boasts a close-knit community. The folk may appear stand-offish to incomers but once you get to know them they have hearts of gold and 'Jethart' has always been at the centre of my life. The BBC rugby commentator Bill McLaren is a fellow Borderer and, I think, he more than understands the love which I have for 'Jethart' and the Border country. Like me, Bill has seen a lot of the world thanks to rugby but, again like me, he always makes a point of getting back to his native Hawick just as quickly as trains and planes will allow.

I was released from Peel Hospital on Christmas Eve and to this day that's about the best Christmas present I've ever had. I was free and, thanks to the superb medical attention which I received, I was cured. My ankle has never bothered me from that day until this and it has taken some punishment over the years on the rugby field. In fact, in light of the injuries which I've suffered in pursuit of the oval ball, some might even say that it's the only part of my body which hasn't been in the wars and put me on the sidelines!

Rugby was in my blood and apart from my family, friends and love of Jed, it has been the dominating force in my life. I have never been more happy than with a rugby ball in my hands.

We were a rugby household. From as far back as I can remember my father was involved with the Jed-Forest club. He was a useful enough centre-cum-wing-forward and my earliest memories are of his filthy kit being brought back for washing and of it drying around the house. He was President of the Jed club in 1994 and, with my Mum, brother Kevin and wife Shona all taking a first-hand interest in the club and the game, it's often seemed that rugby was the sole topic of conversation in the extended Armstrong family.

For almost a quarter of a century my life has been intertwined with the ups and downs of the Jed club. In the Borders, rugby is part of the everyday life of the people. Bill Shankly, the Liverpool FC manager once said that football wasn't a matter of life and death, it was more important than that. Well, that was a particularly stupid thing to say because, of course, it isn't, but I know what he means. In the Borders you're not just playing for your rugby club. You're playing for your town. If the rugby club is doing well then the town feels good about itself. If you are playing for one of the big city clubs then after the game on a Saturday you could just get changed and disappear into the 'real world'. But in the Borders — and every Border town is the same — you can't really escape if you've had a bad game or if the team has lost a game which it should have won. There just is no hiding place. Throughout the next week on the street, in the shops — in fact anywhere — you'll be confronted with your shortcomings and, believe me, every Borderer is an expert on the game — even when they aren't!

But I wouldn't have it any other way. Over the years rugby has provided a sense of community for each of the Border towns and I really can't think of anything else which could have done that in quite the way that rugby has. The Border League comprising Jed, Hawick, Gala, Melrose, Langholm, Selkirk and Kelso was formed at the beginning of the century and it is still the oldest rugby league in the world. It's very much a 'family affair' and much prized in the Borders. Since the arrival of National Leagues in Scotland it doesn't quite have the bite to it which it once did but it is still a trophy that all Border clubs desperately want to win.

Rugby came early to the Borders and the Border clubs are among the oldest in the UK. They were playing rugby at Langholm in 1871, the same year as the world's first international match between Scotland and England at Raeburn Place in Edinburgh. The Hawick club was formed in 1873, followed by Gala in 1876, Melrose in 1877, Kelso in 1884 and Selkirk in 1907. My own club was formed in 1885 although two years before that the young 'callants' of Jed had responded to a challenge from their counterparts in Kelso who had declared that they were going to show Jedburgh 'how to play the game'. Some chance!

Rugby was the perfect game for Borderers. It was rugged and it was played no-holds-barred. Borderers are in lots of ways a race apart. For hundreds of years we lived on the front line in the wars between England and Scotland. And when Border Scots weren't fighting their southern neighbours they just fought amongst themselves. The Border Reivers struck fear into the hearts of the English living south of the Cheviots and many is the head of sheep and cattle that was driven northward in the dead of night. My ancestors even gave the word 'blackmail' to the English language. The Borderers would descend on the likes of Newcastle, Carlisle or Durham and threaten a 'right good howkin' if large quantities of cash and booty were not forthcoming. I never needed much encouragement on Calcutta Cup Saturdays when the opponents were the Auld Enemy!

The Armstrongs were a particularly rumbustious bunch. They really liked to get stuck-in. They caused so much trouble — even to fellow Borderers — that in 1530 the Scottish king James came down from Edinburgh to settle their hash. Johnnie Armstrong of Gilnockie was reckoned to be one of the main ringleaders and the king, with 10,000 men at his back, arranged to meet Johnnie, who had just 50 men with him, at Carlenrig near Teviothead just south of Hawick. Johnnie thought he was being invited along for a 'chat' but without much ado Armstrong of Gilnockie was taken completely by surprise and hanged from a tree which is said to still stand in Teviothead churchyard. Armstrongs have always been careful to watch the blind side ever since!

Those days are remembered each year in all of the Border towns with the Common Ridings and festivals. Mounted supporters follow the town principals on ride-outs to places of historic interest around about. Shona and I have a fine retired hunter and it's the plan that we'll take part in as many of these summer festivals as we can in the years ahead.

My real introduction to the game of rugby took place, as with most Border lads, on a piece of waste ground near my house. In the Borders, rugby is the people's game and it is played on the streets, and on any spare piece of grass, just as football is in the cities. I could never wait to get home from primary school so that I could dump my gear and join the game that was always going on at the Middle Green near my house. Some of the boys that I played with there as a five-year-old, like Gregor McKechnie and Kevin Liddle, went on to play first-class rugby with me for Jed down at Riverside Park. That's the difference between Border sides and those from the cities where club loyalty doesn't appear to be top priority and where player comings and goings begin to look like the soccer transfer market.

We would just improvise with school blazers for goalposts. Conversions never played a big part in these Middle Green games! The boys who played in those games went on to participate in the organised mini-rugby coaching sessions that my dad and a couple of his mates introduced at Riverside Park. The Royal Burgh of Jedburgh isn't a big place and it is one of the smallest of the Border towns. Nevertheless, we are proud of the fact that from such a small catchment area and with not many players to draw from, we have managed to put out sides which have always challenged the best in Scotland. We have managed, often, to play above ourselves because of this community spirit and it was because we have such a small player base on which to build that the club decided that it would take part in the mini-rugby experiment. As a club, what we had to do was to manufacture our own players. Nobody else was going to do it for us. Mini-rugby isn't universally popular in the Borders and at the time of writing they still don't have it in Hawick. In fact, carloads of Hawick boys come down to Jed every Sunday for mini-rugby training. So, I suppose you could say that many future Hawick stars will have got their basic grounding in Jedburgh.

We didn't play rugby in the early years at Howdenburn Primary School in Jedburgh and so I was more or less restricted to the Middle Green games and I wanted more. It was a family laundry crisis which set me on my way to all of the fun — mixed with not a little heartache — that rugby has provided me with.

Weekends revolved around rugby. On Saturdays it would be soup and sandwiches for lunch and then off to Riverside to watch Jed. First of all we used to go down to watch Dad and then the family would turn out en masse because I was a ball-boy. Jed were in the Scottish second division then and so I never really got the opportunity to watch the big international stars in operation. But Roy Laidlaw was just starting to make a name for himself around this time and so even though I was just five or six, in my ball-boy phase, I saw him develop from promising youngster to fully-fledged international. Of course I had no way of knowing it at the time but I would eventually profit from the vast store of knowledge that he had picked up along the way.

Sundays meant mini-rugby. Kevin and I would go down with Dad and his pals and generally just muck about as the bigger boys went through their paces. Invariably we would get absolutely filthy. Mum got so fed up of her two sons being brought home covered head to feet in glaur that eventually she said that if we were going down to Riverside every Sunday then we would be as well to get ourselves kitted out. We got the shorts and the shirts and the tracksuits and the boots: we were well chuffed.

I was officially a couple of years too young to take part but I liked getting mucked in with the older lads. Eventually, they let me take part in actual games and then I was picked to go in the side and to travel to mini-rugby tournaments.

I was always a scrum-half. I must have looked like a scrum-half from day one and that was where I was put. I had always liked mixing it with the bigger lads and so the position suited me fine. Once, they tried to move me from scrum-half and I left the field in floods of tears.

These were the very early days of mini-rugby and it wasn't nearly as popular as it is now. Accordingly there weren't many tournaments for us to go to but I do recall a tourney that we went to at Berwick. We won and we each got a certificate signed by Andy Irvine. When you're only eight that really means something to you and I've tried to remember how I felt then whenever I'm asked to do something with rugby youngsters these days.

Strangely enough, though, my earliest rugby memories aren't really of playing at all. The earliest picture that comes back to me is of 'ball-boying' at Jed Sevens. It always seemed to me that half of Scotland had arrived at Riverside Park. The stand and the embankments would be packed and folk would bring travelling rugs and picnic baskets and sit around the touchlines. I used to get so carried away with the play that I would be standing up on the touchline and the folk behind couldn't see. Even yet the Jed crowd isn't known for its inability to call a spade a spade and they would be shouting: 'Will ye bloody sit doon? Ah cannae see the game.'

So ball-boy at Riverside was my introduction to what I thought was the real big-time. But mini-rugby was where I learned the basic skills of rugby football. I would recommend it to any parent and, for the survival and well-being of the game itself, that must be where the future lies. The schools don't seem to be taking much of an interest in sport these days and it has come down to the clubs to foster and train young talent.

Everything that I know about rugby can be traced back to those Sunday sessions at Riverside Park. Since then I've played with and against the top players in the world and I've been coached by some of the world's top coaches. But mini-rugby was where I had the basics drummed into me. I watched the game at Riverside on the Saturday and then I couldn't wait for Sunday to arrive so that I could get the ball into my hands and have a run about. That's where I learned to tackle, pass, kick and when to go for the break. Mini-rugby was certainly good for me.

However, there is a down side. The behaviour of some parents and the coaches leaves a lot to be desired. They stand on the touchlines screaming and bawling at the boys. They take it far too seriously. I was presenting prizes at one mini-rugby tournament and I was disgusted by some of the things that I saw and heard. Mini-rugby should be played for enjoyment. It should be enjoyed by the boys and it should be enjoyed by the mothers and fathers. When a kid is being yelled at then it's no longer an enjoyable experience and that kid will, eventually, be lost to the game. At that level, and even up through the grades, the boys should be taught the basics and then they should be taught that it's a fun thing.

If I ever take up coaching then it's likely that I'll do so at semi-junior level and I'll be coaching the boys first of all to have fun. Then if they're enjoying their rugby and getting the basics right, the results will follow. There'll be plenty of pressure rugby later but at that age, and certainly lower down the age scale, the game should be competitive, sure, but it should be played for fun.

Fun wasn't the word which came immediately to mind when, in 1975, my link with Jed was about to be severed. Dad had been promoted and was moving to his insurance company's office in Berwick. We moved to nearby Coldstream which is about as far south as you can go in Scotland without falling over into England. In fact the River Tweed, which represents the Border, runs alongside the town. The move meant leaving behind my pals in Jed but it could have been worse, we could have crossed the Tweed and moved into Sassenach country itself!

Coldstream was fine but to my dismay I discovered that they didn't play rugby at all in my new school. I was beginning to suffer withdrawal symptoms but things were not as bad as they might have been because every Sunday the Armstrong family would climb into the car and motor back to Jed for mini-rugby. That way, too, I was able to keep in touch with all my friends back home — I always looked upon Jed as 'home' even when we weren't living there — and to continue my rugby education.

Simultaneously I was playing football at primary school in Coldstream and despite the fact that I wasn't much interested in the round-ball game I made a useful enough centre-forward or right winger and I have a very distinct memory that I was actually picked to play in a Northumberland schoolboy trial match. I know Northumberland is in England and that Coldstream is in Scotland — just — but that is what happened. The match itself was cancelled and I never got the chance to show what I was capable of. I enjoyed playing football but I just saw it as a pastime. Rugby was different. Even at that age I thought it was my life.

After primary school at Coldstream I moved on to Berwickshire High School at Duns. This was more to my liking because we were back into rugby again. They must have been just introducing this alien game into the school when I arrived because I recall that I was about the only boy who could play the game. By strange coincidence one of our first fixtures was against my old mates at Jedburgh Grammar School. We were so bad at Duns that some of the Jed boys were put into our team to get something like an equal game going. Jethart humped us. I was secretly chuffed. Good old Jed.

Berwickshire High School now has a well-deserved reputation for the excellence of its rugby but in my day the game was in its infancy there. There was an old guy who coached at the school, Archie McCulloch, and he singled me out for special tuition. He took me under his wing. He built the teams up. I was only there for a year or so until further promotion for my dad took the family northwards and across the Forth Road Bridge to Dunfermline. But we continued our regular Sunday pilgrimages back to Jedburgh for the mini-rugby. As I look back I realise that I have a lot to be thankful for. My parents were determined that, despite our 'exile' from the Borders, Kevin and I should not lose sight of our roots. If we hadn't made these regular trips back to Jed then I am absolutely certain that my rugby career would not have worked out as it did.

We were in Dunfermline when the time came for mc to say cheerio to mini-rugby. We travelled down from the Kingdom of Fife to Prestonpans in East Lothian. We met up with the Jed lads to take part in the Preston Lodge RFC mini tournament at Pennypit Park. I knew that it was to be my last tourney and I wanted to go out on a 'high'. But it was to be the lowest of lows. The pride of Jed found themselves banned and we were slung out of the competition for playing an over-age 'ringer'.

We were into the final and due, I think, to play Royal High, when their coach made a formal complaint to the organisers that we were playing an over-age kid. As boys do, we had been blethering to the boys from other towns and somebody had asked about ages. Age is a big thing with young kids and there are always stories in age groups, whatever the age, about so-and-so being too old to take part. I think, particularly, of some of the French schoolboy internationals. Some of their players look like they've been around for a guid few summers!

In any event, the 'culprit' in our side was Duncan Brown. Duncan was a big lad right enough but we were convinced that we had done nothing wrong. It turned out that there had been a heated exchange over eligibility. There was a different interpretation in the Borders to that in the cities. It made a difference of only a year or so, so far as the boys were concerned, but after a heated 'steward's inquiry' at Pennypit Park we were ejected. The Jed parents and coaches were absolutely furious. They never even stayed for their complimentary tea! They marched straight on to their bus and buzzed off home. Kevin, my dad and I got into the car and drove back over the Forth to Dunfermline. I didn't appreciate it at the time but that was to be my last link with Jed rugby for four years. And after so many years of so much fun it was a sour note on which to end.

The Kingdom of Fife, with St Andrews on the coast and scores more golf courses scattered throughout the county, is more noted for its golf than its Rugby Union football. A hotbed of rugby it isn't. Dunfermline High School, which was to be my next port of educational call, wasn't noted for its rugby prowess either but two fellow exiles from the Borders were doing their level best to put that right. Colin McKay, who played at scrum-half for North and Midlands, was in charge of rugby and another Hawick man, Greg Chisholm, was also on the staff, chemistry I think, and took a keen interest in the deeds of the rugby team. It was Greg's misfortune that as my form master he had to look after my educational progress in the first couple of years at Dunfermline. One conversation in particular stands out. I had to go to see him in order to choose what subjects I was going to take for O-levels. As I've said, I was never a keen scholar and the chat with Mr Chisholm was pretty much one-way traffic. By which I mean Greg would say what about this or that subject and I would say that I wasn't too keen. Eventually, in exasperation, I said to him: 'I'll tell you what. I'm not much interested in anything else. I'll just stay on to play rugby!'

Even a rugby-daft Hawick man has to draw the line somewhere and my not entirely in jest plea was turned down flat.

Throughout my days at school I had only one aim and that was to escape as quickly as possible. I had already made up my mind what I wanted to do when I gained my freedom and that was to work on a farm. Some boys wanted to be engine drivers or airline pilots but I knew what I wanted. And that is eventually what I did.

The town of Dunfermline itself I found very strange at first. It has an Abbey like Jedburgh but there the similarities ended. Compared to Jed and Coldstream, Dunfermline seemed huge. On my first morning at the High School there, one of my classmates looked me in the eye and said he was going to give me 'a hammering at break time'. To put it mildly I was a bit startled. I was an incomer with a broad Borders dialect and some of my classmates had trouble understanding what I was saying. Then the PE department found out that I could play rugby and I went virtually straight into the first XV alongside all of the bigger boys from the senior school. Once I was into the first XV the two or three boys in my form who had been giving me a bit of a hard time just backed off.

At the same time as my career in full-time education was going downhill my rugby was beginning to pick up. Colin McKay really began to push me along and I made the North and Midlands Under-15 side. I had hamstring trouble as a 15-year-old and Mr McKay must have thought that I was worth persevering with because he got me in to see the Hearts FC physio at Tynecastle. He got me sorted out and back on to the rugby pitch. Other rugby contemporaries at Dunfermline were Martin Scott, who won a couple of caps at hooker during Scotland's 1992 Australian tour; Dean Spiddle, who went on to become a more than useful golfer; and my stand-off, Jimmy Govan, who went on to play cricket for Scotland.

I was also playing a fair bit of golf during my period in Fife. We stayed almost next door to the Pitreavie Golf Club and during the holidays Kevin and I would sneak on to the course at the second hole and play 16 holes before diving back through the hedge at the seventeenth. We liked the golf well enough. It was the course fees that we objected to. Pitreavie was a good course and we couldn't afford the price of a round. These games with Kevin were really competitive affairs. We both hate to be beaten and we would really hammer it out over 16 holes. Looking back, I think we both had a bit of talent for the game. I liked it and might dust down the clubs and get back out on to the golf links once I've retired from rugby. This time, though, I'll pay the green fees!

Kevin is a couple of years younger than me but from as far back as I can remember — and no matter what the game was — we seem to have been in competition with each other. He's a flanker and he's come right up through the rugby grades with me and we played as team-mates at Riverside Park. In 1993 Kevin went on Scotland's tour to Western Samoa, Fiji and Tonga. He's had more than his fair share of injuries and so hasn't got the wider recognition that he deserves but everything that Kevin has achieved in rugby has given me almost as much pleasure as anything that I've done myself.

At school, I was as happy as a pig in glaur when the rugby season was on but the summer months dragged as I counted down the days to my release. As I've said, I had known what I wanted to do since I was knee-high to Roy Laidlaw! The open-air life on the farm, where you were your own boss and working by the sweat of your own brow was my goal. Before I left Dunfermline HS I had been offered a Youth Training Scheme place at Rawflats Farm, near Jedburgh. It was ideal. It meant that I could return to my beloved Borderland and that I could lodge with my gran and grandpa Paxton who stayed on the neighbouring Pinnacle Farm where my grandfather was the farm steward.

Even my first job at Rawflats couldn't put me off. I was handed a 'knapsack' sprayer and told to go and spread weedkiller on a 40-acre field. I can't speak for the weeds but it almost killed me! It took me a day and a half to cover the ground and at the end of it I was absolutely knackered. However, I was 15 years old, I was back in the Borders, I was free from school and my real rugby education was just about to get under way.

CHAPTER 2

SCHOOL OF HARD KNOCKS

My Education Continues

IT BEGAN with a phone call to my gran. Jed Thistle were short of a player and they wanted me to play for them. I was chuffed. I played for the Thistle in a friendly before the start of the semi-junior leagues and it must have gone all right because I was soon a regular in the side.

Semi-junior rugby was a big step up from what I had been used to at school and it was the ideal preparation for what lay ahead. It was superbly competitive with a keenly contested league involving semi-junior sides from the other Border towns. There was also family tradition involved because my dad had captained the Thistle in his younger days. In fact, in 1964, he was the first Thistle captain to take the side down to Wales for the biennial game against New Tredegar on the eve of the Wales *v* Scotland international. I followed in his footsteps as captain in 1983 and the tradition was maintained when Kevin was made captain two years later.

As a 15-year-old I found semi-junior rugby a tough school in which to make my mark. It's an Under-18 grade and there's a big difference physically between a 15-year-old and an 18-year-old. I was constantly being confronted by boys who were much bigger than me — you might say that nothing much has changed! But it was a great environment in which to learn. I really enjoyed my time with the Thistle and the education didn't end with rugby. It was at the Thistle that I learned how to drink — and how not to drink! — and generally the Thistle was an important part of the growing-up process. We had a very successful team. We won the Digital Scottish Youth Trophy which operated like a premiership bringing together the top teams from the local leagues all over Scotland. It was a good system which meant that from day one you were playing hard, competitive rugby.

It was out of the Thistle club that I was picked for my first Scottish representative game. I played for Scotland Under-18s against Scottish Schools at Murrayfield. It wasn't exactly a dream début. It was a bitterly cold day and it lashed with rain throughout. Midway through the second half I was just wishing that it was all over. Andrew 'Rip' Redpath of Melrose was my number 8 and he was doing a lot of pick-ups from the base of the scrum. I wasn't too sure of myself in those days otherwise I would have told him to pack it in. In fact I probably did tell him to pack it in but telling 'Rip' something and him actually doing something about it is another thing entirely.

I was being left with all of the useless ball and I had a bit of a stinker so it didn't come as too much of a surprise when I was dropped after just one outing. Rob Young of Biggar, and later Selkirk, got my place. I knew that I hadn't played particularly well but, nevertheless, it hurt. It was the first and hopefully the last time that I've ever been dropped and it brought home to me that I couldn't just take things for granted and that if I really wanted to progress in the game then I would have to become more focused. I toured Sweden with the Scotland Under-18 side and that gave me a taste of the possibilities that were open to me if I really stuck in. Even at that early stage I wasn't a dedicated trainer. I still looked upon rugby as a serious hobby and didn't want to devote my entire life to it. But when I did train I put more effort into it in an attempt to make sure that the selectors didn't think that they could discard me again.

Even in those early days my rugby philosophy was that it was a hobby and a game to be played for fun. Later on, when I made the national side, I just couldn't believe the effort that some boys had to put in to keep their places. They were out training for a couple of hours every single day of their lives. That wasn't for me. Twice a week with the club and a game on Saturday was the target that I set myself. Mind you, when I do train I don't go in for half measures. I train until it hurts. But, for me, the biggest single thing about progressing in the game is mental attitude.

Folk think that I'm a laid-back kind of person who just takes life as it comes along. Off the field that's probably true. But once I pull on a rugby shirt then I give one hundred and one per cent every time, for every team that I play for. I also knew, within myself, after I had been around the national side for a couple of seasons, that I was better than every single scrum-half that I ever played against. I didn't boast about it. In fact I never even spoke about it. But I knew that whenever I stood on a rugby pitch I was going to be better than the other guy. Maybe, in reality, I wasn't but I had to have that inner confidence, that self-belief if I was going to withstand the intensity of the game at international level. I'll go into this in more detail in a later chapter but the self-belief thing was a lesson I learned the first time I played against Pierre Berbizier in Paris. After that experience I vowed that I would never again go into the game thinking myself second-best or giving the other guy an inch.

But all of that was in the future. With the Thistle, despite the fact that they thought I was playing OK, I still didn't have self-belief. I was always worrying about my passing or my kicking. I was worrying about whether I was good enough to do this or that. Often after a game I would ask my father what he had thought about my performance. He would point me in the right direction or tell me not to be so daft. He was invaluable to my development as a player. He never pushed me or became one of those fathers who get worked up on the touchline but he was always there to offer advice and, more importantly, he never pulled the wool over my eyes. If I had played a stinker then he told me and offered encouragement and if I had played well then he gave me the praise that everybody needs to feel good about themselves.

Now and then Roy Laidlaw would appear at Thistle training. Of course Roy was still Scotland's scrum-half at the time and he was playing for Jed-Forest. They trained and played at the same time as us and so he never really had the opportunity to have a good look at us on a regular basis. He did come down to our pitch, overlooked by the ancient abbey, on a couple of occasions, and he talked me through my service and my kicking.

He must have seen something that he liked because during my second season with the semi-juniors he tried to get me along to Riverside Park a year early. I decided that it was better for me to stay where I was for the time being and didn't go.

Eventually I made the transition to the senior club in 1986. I played for a year in the second XV while Roy was in the firsts. Roy was invaluable at this time. After training was finished he would spend half an hour with me on my own. I would practise passing balls against the stand so that I could get the accuracy and speed up to scratch. Later, before Craig Chalmers and I played our first international together, Roy had us down at Riverside for an hour just running through the whole routine. Roy never tried to make me into a Laidlaw Mark 2. He was his kind of player and I was mine but all the tricks of the trade that he passed on after such a brilliant international career were absolutely invaluable in my own progress through the ranks. Throughout my time in the Jed seconds I was his understudy. Whenever he was away playing a representative game I would take over. Then it would be back to the seconds where I was enjoying my rugby nevertheless.

During my second season at the club, when we were fighting to avoid relegation, I was actually drafted into the first XV at scrum-half and Roy played fly-half. That didn't go down too well with the national selectors, though, who preferred to see Roy playing in his regular international berth.

I recall one particular occasion early on when I was in the seconds and Roy was playing stand-off. I couldn't consider myself to be a regular in the first XV but on this particular day I was desperate to play. Jed were playing Hawick in a Boxing Day game at Mansfield Park. This was the real big-time so far as I was concerned, big crowds and a lot of town pride at stake. I sat beside the phone waiting for the call to tell me that I was being promoted from the 'twos'. But the call never came. They had drafted somebody else into the side. I was gutted. I consoled myself by thinking that I wasn't a regular so I hadn't been dropped but it was a real sickener nonetheless.

It would be around this time, 1987 or thereabouts, that I first made the acquaintance of Craig Minto Chalmers. He was playing for Melrose 'A' and I was playing for Jed 'A'. I suppose we must have played against each other at some point but he never made much of an impact on me. Then we were chosen as the half-backs for the South District Union side, which is made up of the top players from the Border junior clubs and the second XVs of the senior clubs in the area.

We played together against an Edinburgh District Union side and then, a wee while later, against our counterparts in Glasgow. That game was played in the mud pool at Hughenden and we really got it together. I don't really know why we got on so well together. Without sounding corny, it just seemed that we were made for each other. 'Chic' and I hit it off from the word go and we've come up through the grades together. I know his game inside out and he has the same kind of relationship with me. Half-back partnerships are made in some kind of rugby heaven. You have to have an absolute understanding with your other half. On TV Bill McLaren always used to refer to established half-back partnerships — the Hasties and Chisholms or Laidlaws and Rutherfords — as the 'ham and eggs'. And that's just about a perfect way of describing it. The partnership should be so close that you really shouldn't be able to think of one without the other.

By the end of 1987 I had become a regular in the Jed first XV. I had already represented Scotland at Under-18, Youth and Under-21 level and my rugby education was progressing apace.

I won a couple of Scotland 'B' caps in 1988 even before I had played for the South of Scotland senior side. I scored a hat-trick in a 37–0 win over Italy then played against the French in France.

I knew that Roy was thinking about calling it a day and I was determined to succeed him in the Scotland side. The heir-apparent was Hawick's Greig Oliver. He had sat on the bench on countless occasions and was ahead of me in the pecking order. As things turned out I followed Roy straight into the national side. He retired at the end of the 1988 Five Nations tournament and I won my first cap the following autumn against Australia. It was bad luck on Greig. Maybe if he had got a couple of games in a Scotland shirt after Roy's retirement then I would never have got a look-in but he didn't and that's just the way the cookie crumbles.

Because of this rivalry between Greig and me, I always looked upon Hawick *v* Jed games as something special. I was always wanting to put one over on him and he was the same with me. He was a tricky player, left-handed so more difficult to play against. Whenever I was up against Greig I always gave him a lot of respect but he was a player that I knew I could get at. Some scrum-halves are like that. You can get them niggly and their game goes off. I always knew that I could get to Greig and that his game would suffer as a result. There was, though, one match at Mansfield where the Hawick pack had given our boys a bit of a working-over and Greig was outshining me. After the game my father said: 'Well, Greig had the better of you today.' I knew he had but I would never have admitted it. I just logged it away to make sure that the next time we met I would end up on top.

I'm still a great supporter of the Border League. It's the oldest rugby competition in the world and it still deserves its place in the calendar today. If your club can't win the National Championship then it's good to be able to have a crack at its Border equivalent. In addition, Border League matches are all local derbies. The players have all known each other since they were kids and have been playing each other since then as well. There are old rivalries and old scores to be settled and, for me, a

Border derby will always mean more than a game against one of the top city sides.

The Jed *v* Kelso game was always a bit of a grudge game and I can remember the first time I played at Poynder Park not long after I'd made my breakthrough into the first XV. I was lying trapped on the wrong side of a ruck and I had a worm's eye view of the Kelso captain Gary Callander bearing down on me at a rate of knots. Gary was a ruthless bugger and I just knew that he was homing in on me. I just closed my eyes and waited for the worst. Then I felt a hand protecting my head and looked up to see Eric Paxton, the Kelso flanker — who luckily just also happens to be my cousin — and he said: 'Git yer heid oot the bloody way or it'll be kicked clean off yer shoulders!' It's not often that you have the luxury of a relative looking after your interests from the opposition side of the fence but I'm sure glad that Packie was around that day.

It's only seven or eight years since I began playing senior rugby with Jed but, even in that short space of time, I've noticed a difference in attitude among some Border players. When I first started, guys like the ex-Scotland forwards Jim Aitken, Alan Tomes, Tom Smith, Alister Campbell and Callander himself were still around. They were rough, tough and uncompromising players. They were quite ruthless. We used to look upon some of the city sides as being a bunch of softies. But now the tables seem to have been turned. City sides have got the upper hand for the moment and they're just as ruthless as the Border sides of the past decade used to be. We're also struggling in the Borders to keep our players on their home patch. People move away to the cities for jobs and to college and university, and the pool of players that Border clubs can choose from seems to get smaller every season.

I've loved playing for Jed. I can't imagine ever having played for another club. You're playing for your town. If you have a good game then everybody you meet on the street is congratulating you. Mind you, if you've not played so well then they're not slow to tell you that either. A story which perfectly sums up the down-to-earth attitude of Border folk is one which

Roy tells against himself. He was a member of Scotland's 1984 Grand Slam side — and with my efforts in 1990 that's quite a double for Jed by the way — and on the Monday after all the weekend's jubilation and adulation he was back in Jed working away as an electrician rewiring the public toilets. Now that kind of thing really keeps your feet on the ground.

The one thing which is missing from my store of rugby memorabilia is a Jed Sevens medal. The Jed tournament has a unique atmosphere. It's on a much smaller scale than Melrose, of course, but it attracts a huge crowd, good guest sides and not insubstantial sponsorship. But every time since Tennents have become involved as the major sponsors I have been injured. It's now my ambition to keep plugging away until I've got a Jed medal. After I've achieved that I'll call it a day. But not before. I may still be playing when I hit 40!

CHAPTER 3

OPENING AGAINST AUSTRALIA

International Début

AS 1988 got under way there was one man standing between me and the Scottish cap that I so desperately wanted. Roy Laidlaw, my Riverside Park mentor, had never said anything to me directly but the press were hinting that this was to be his last season. Roy's understudy was Hawick's Greig Oliver. He had understudied Roy so often that he must have had corns on his backside from all that sitting on the bench.

Greig was a first-rate player but he was unlucky that he was on the scene at the same time as Roy. We had some rare old tussles whenever our clubs met. He was a difficult guy to play against because, as I've said, he was left-handed and left-footed. Although you're supposed to be able to kick equally well with either foot you wouldn't be human if you didn't favour one. Most scrum-halves favour the right side and so that was just something extra that you had to watch out for when you were playing Greig.

Just after New Year, 1988, I was picked to sit on the bench at the National Trial. The main contest was still between Greig and Roy but then fate stepped in and, for once, the fates were in my favour.

Greig came off with a dead leg at half-time and I took his place. It was tough on Greig but, as I was to discover as my

Scotland career progressed, these things happen. So my first appearance at Murrayfield, pretty deserted though it was, was in direct opposition to Roy. I enjoyed the experience immensely and it was all part of the learning process for me. At the first scrum the ball shot out at a bad angle for Roy. I sniped away at him and snatched the ball from under his nose. Nothing was said but he gave me an old-fashioned look and at the next scrum he came round so far offside that it looked like he had been studying the Fin Calder coaching manual. He dug the ball out from under my nose and he had made his point. I had 'done' him and he was making damn sure that I wasn't going to do him again. After that I didn't have much of a game!

I was just a youngster and pretty naïve. I only had half a game and it's pretty difficult to get yourself on to the pace when you're suddenly pitched in midway through a match.

As I've said, I didn't know it at the time but this was, indeed, the start of Roy's last international season. He retired after the final Five Nations game against England at Murrayfield. It was an appalling game which ended in a 9–6 defeat for Scotland. England had played negatively from start to finish and Roy deserved a better end to his international career than that.

I reckoned that Greig was still ahead of me in the pecking order and so far as most observers were concerned he was going to be the logical successor once Roy had gone. It was lucky for me, but desperately bad luck for Greig, that he had to come off hurt in the trial. That allowed the Scotland selectors to make a direct comparison between me and Greig. I have always thought that if Greig had made it to the Scotland side instead of me then I would have had a heck of a job dislodging him.

However, I had played for Scotland at Youth, Under-18 and Under-21 level and so I didn't just appear out of the blue. I was already something of a known quantity to the Scotland selectors. I had played a couple of games for Scotland 'B', scoring a hat-trick against the Italians at Aberdeen and doing all right for the 'B' team despite being beaten by France in St Andrews. These games were all part of the learning process for me. It's important that a player climbs the ladder just one rung at a time. There are players who are pitched into international rugby too soon for their own good. At the top of the rugby pyramid it's a very different ball game from club or district rugby and ideally you should have a treasure store of experience to fall back on when the going gets tough.

To my mind the reason why the talented Gala man Gregor Townsend struggled when he first came into the Scotland side was because far too much was expected of him too soon. The Scotland management wanted him in the side before, in my opinion, he was ready. He should have had another couple of seasons learning his trade in the 'A' side before being thrown in at the deep end with a full Scotland cap.

The Australians were in Scotland at the end of 1988 and I was desperately keen to show what I could do. It was still touch-and-go as to whether the selectors would go for Greig or me. I was on tenterhooks as they deliberated in Edinburgh. I was still working on the farm and I had left the house before the mail arrived in the morning. I couldn't really keep my mind on the job and I sprinted home at lunchtime to see if the postman had been. Just as I got there the postie, Ernie Tooley, a good Jed supporter, arrived bearing the letter from Murrayfield. Ernie had seen 'Scottish Rugby Union' marked on the outside of the envelope and so he waited as I tore it open. He didn't need to ask when he saw the size of the grin on my face.

The letter informed me that I had been selected to play for Scotland against the Australian tourists at Murrayfield on Saturday, 19 November. I was chuffed. Secretly, though, I was more than a little apprehensive. I had played against the Wallabies for the South of Scotland and we had been absolutely humped. I had found the going extremely tough and in addition I had injured my shoulder. If it hadn't been my first cap then I would probably have cried off but I banked on the shoulder mending in time and, in any case, I would have played with my arm in a sling so keen was I to get that first outing for Scotland.

My gran and grandpa weren't on the telephone at Rawflats and I was desperate to phone my mum and dad. I nipped along to a neighbouring farm steading bursting to tell them my news. But by the time I got through they had already heard it on the radio. They were as pleased for me as I was. When I went back to work I was really full of myself. I had put a lot of hard graft into my rugby and now I had done it. I had been selected to wear the number 9 shirt for Scotland. I had the cows for company that afternoon and they didn't give a damn. It didn't make the slightest bit of difference to them that I wasn't the same Gary Armstrong that I had been in the morning. Every now and then my attention would be distracted as daydreams of that blue jersey and the Murrayfield roar entered my head. The cows weren't impressed in the slightest and my daydream would be rudely interrupted as one or other of the beasts gave me a nudge or a sly kick. There's no chance of becoming big-headed when your companions on the day that you're picked to play for Scotland is a herd of coos!

The Scotland team in which I made by debut read: Gavin Hastings, Matt Duncan, Scott Hastings, Keith Robertson, Iwan Tukalo, Richard Cramb, me, David Sole, Gary Callander, Iain Milne, Alister Campbell, Damian Cronin, Derek White, John Jeffrey and Iain Paxton.

In retrospect I suppose that it was a team in transition. Iain Milne and Keith Robertson were winning their forty-first caps and Iain Paxton had played 35 times for Scotland. At the other end of the scale were me and Richard Cramb, my half-back partner for the afternoon who was winning only his fourth cap. And in-between were the likes of David Sole and the Hastings boys who had come into the side together two years previously. Gary Callander captained the side from hooker. It was to be his last game for Scotland. He was another of those guys, like Greig Oliver, who suffered from being around at the same time as one of the greats. Gary, who was a first-class player with a very astute tactical awareness, got his breakthrough into the side only after Colin Deans had retired. Gary had sat on the bench umpteen times but by the time that Colin had called it a day, with a then Scottish record haul of 52 caps, time was running out for Callander.

Until I was called into the Scotland set-up for the Wallabies game I had never met Richard Cramb. He was an Exile or, as they were still called then, an Anglo. He played for Harlequins and he had been called into the Scottish 1987 World Cup party when John Rutherford had been invalided home with a serious knee injury. He had played once as a replacement during the World Cup and had won a couple of caps during the Five Nations Championship which followed. I didn't know much about him and wouldn't get the chance to put that right because he never played for Scotland again after that game.

The New Zealand News Under-21 Youth side played their Scottish counterparts as a curtain-raiser to our game against the Wallabies and my future international partner was to be found within the Scotland Under-21 ranks. By the time the next Five Nations championship came around Craig Chalmers would have left the Under-21s behind and would be making his debut in the big side.

Like every new cap before me the thing that was uppermost in my mind was to make sure that I didn't let anyone down. It was great to be in the same team as guys like The Bear and Keith Robertson. I knew that I would be able to cope but as the new boy in the class I still felt that I had to show all the older boys that I had been worthy of my selection.

That was also Ian McGeechan's first game as Scotland coach. Over the next few years our rugby paths would become intertwined. He made a big impression on me. Ian is one of the world's most respected coaches. He went on to coach the Lions to a series win over the Australians in 1989 and to come within a dodgy refereeing decision of doing the same thing to the Kiwis in 1993. He also masterminded England's Grand Slam downfall in 1990 so a bright future was in store for him. Even then in 1988 I could see that he was something special. He didn't shout and bawl like some coaches did. He was quiet and methodical and you knew exactly what it was that he wanted. He was very kind to me. He said that I was just to play my normal game but, above all else, I was just to go out and enjoy myself.

In the Murrayfield dressing-room beforehand I was as nervous as a kitten and the game itself just passed in a blur. During the first five minutes I took a knock to the head. I don't think that I was concussed or anything like that but I was very definitely dazed and for some of the time I was running around in a haze. My hearing was also badly affected and every time the crowd cheered I got an echo inside my head. It was a weird sensation. Even allowing for the fact that I wasn't quite all there for some of the time, I found my first taste of international rugby an exhausting experience. The pace of an international game is something else again. You hardly ever get the chance to take a breather and mentally the game is yards faster than even a top-level club game. You have to make your decisions so much quicker because boys are closing you down in about half the time it would take in club rugby.

Half-time arrived and I thought we had just been playing for ten minutes. You are trying so hard and concentrating to the exclusion of everything else that normal time just doesn't have any meaning.

Afterwards I couldn't remember a thing about the game. For me it had just passed in a streak of blue and gold. We were gubbed 32–13 and I don't think we played particularly well. The Australian skipper Nick Farr-Jones was my immediate opponent that afternoon but, to be honest, he didn't make much of an impression on me. Certainly at that stage in his career, he wasn't one of those guys who you felt was an outstanding scrum-half or even an outstanding competitor. Later on I would have my hands full during my first tussle with Pierre Berbizier of France and that left an indelible mark on my memory. But with Farr-Jones there is nothing.

Everybody seemed to have been quite happy with my performance but I wasn't. It's only when you get back home and watch the game on video that you really begin to register what took place. When you are actually playing in an international match — and especially your first one — you are concentrating so hard and, in a physical sense, so pushing your body to the limit that you don't have time to form an opinion as to how you've played. When I watched myself in the Australian game I was kicking myself for some of the silly things that I had done but that is all part of the learning process. You have to profit from your mistakes by making sure that you don't do the same silly things again.

After the game I was asking my dad if he thought I had done enough to be re-selected. He told me not to worry because I was a certainty. That was just his opinion, though, and obviously he was biased. That worry about whether you have done enough to merit re-selection is something that never really leaves you. If there is a rival breathing down your neck then that really keeps you on your toes and, certainly as far as I'm concerned, that old adage about a player only being as good as his last game is true. I never took re-selection for granted and every time I went out to play for Scotland I felt that I was playing for my place in the side. Maybe when Scotland were going through that black patch of nine games without a win there were too many players taking their places for granted. Playing with a bit of fear in your heart is no bad thing. Ideally there should be competition for every place in the side. It's just the same in football where managers buy players in order to put pressure on the established stars. Everybody plays better when they know that there's a ready-made replacement lurking in the wings.

Back in 1988/89 I had a long time to wait to see whether or not I was back in the side. There was the International Trial at Murrayfield in early January and this time I was in the senior Blues side.

Then they put me out of my misery by selecting me for the opening Five Nations game against Wales. Craig Chalmers was also in the side. It was to be his first cap and my second. The boys from the Borders were finding their international feet together. Very early on we were being compared to Roy Laidlaw and John

Rutherford but that was just ridiculous. Compared to them we were just novices. What I would say, though, is that from very early on in our playing relationship we just clicked. I have absolutely no idea why that should be but I always felt comfortable playing with Chic outside me and he, obviously, was happy with my part in the partnership. We had first played together, as I've said, for the South District Union and right away we hit it off. In absolutely non-technical language, I just felt that he stood in the right places for me. I didn't have to look around to see where he was because I just knew where he would be in any given situation. We were on the same wave-length because if I had been in his shoes, that's where I would have stood as well.

Our first game together in full Scottish colours was that outing against Wales. We must have been doing something right because we won 23–7. Craig scored a try and kicked a drop-goal and I scored a try. Finlay Calder was captain for the first time that day and, along with Chic, the other new caps were Sean Lineen, Kenny Milne and Chris Gray. I was a bit apprehensive about Finlay. He would give you the rough edge of his tongue if you dropped a ball or weren't concentrating at training sessions. I asked Chic how he got on with Fin and Chic just said, 'Och don't pay any heed to the old bugger. Just let it go in one ear and out the other.' But our early impressions of Finlay were totally wrong. He was a superb captain and a player who led by example. Over the years he made a point of looking after me on the pitch if some of the opposition forwards started getting stroppy.

I think, too, that a word or two about Sean would be appropriate here. He had come over from New Zealand really just to see a bit of the world. He had played rugby in Wales and he landed up at the Boroughmuir Club in Edinburgh. When he was chosen to play for Scotland — by virtue of some long lost Hebridean grandfather – there were those who said that he was just a carpetbagger who wasn't good enough to get a game for New Zealand and so had come over to Scotland to chance his arm here. I never believed that was the case and I still believe that Sean has been great for Scottish rugby. After that afternoon at Murrayfield he would go on to win 29 caps and set up a world-record centre partnership with Scott Hastings.

There are others, though, who don't come into the category which Lineen occupies. For instance, I would never have given a Scottish cap to John Allan. Maybe I'm misjudging him but I never felt that John had made a real commitment to Scotland. He arrived from South Africa which at that time was still in the international wilderness and he threw in his lot with us on account of having been born in Glasgow before moving out to South Africa as a youngster. He got his first cap on tour in New Zealand and played throughout the 1991 World Cup. I thought that he had an eye for the main chance and I always suspected that just as soon as South Africa was readmitted to the international arena then he would be off.

The other guy who I put in this category is the New Zealander Dale McIntosh. He is of Maori stock and is a Kiwi through and through. Playing out of the Welsh club Pontypridd, McIntosh won a couple of Scotland 'A' caps in 1993 and 1994. As a back-row forward he was getting rave reviews but then he got injured and his progress up the ladder was halted. He has since thrown his hat into the Welsh ring but finds himself stymied there because of their rule which states that he cannot play for a Welsh representative side until six years have elapsed from the time that he represented another country.

Somebody has to make a stand somewhere about who is eligible to play for Scotland and other international nations. If the Scottish Rugby Union had gone ahead with the stupid idea of selecting people on the basis of a 12-month residential ruling then I think Scottish internationalists of bygone days would have been birlin' in their graves. With only 15,000 players compared to England's 250,000 we may be hard up but not that hard up surely. I know how much a Scottish cap has meant to me and I know how much hard work has gone into it. The SRU were quite right to back-track on the daft residential ruling. I can tell you that if they hadn't and the Scottish side had been filled with mercenaries from a' the airts then I for one would never have been back at Murrayfield.

My first season in the international game was also my introduction to the glittering world of after-dinner banquets. There are two prerequisites for surviving the banquet season — a strong bladder and a cast-iron liver. With Scotland the format was that after the game we would travel by bus to the Carlton Highland Hotel in the centre of Edinburgh. We would get changed into our evening wear and then nip round to the Mitre Bar in the Royal Mile for a few pints. Then we would go on to the SRU president's reception back at the hotel and all of this was before we had even got to the dinner itself.

With experience you learned to pace yourself but when you first get into the side you are very much the new boy at school and it is oh so easy to find yourself falling by the wayside.

These dinners after internationals are, for me, what the game is all about. You can knock lumps out of each other for 80 minutes on the pitch but afterwards you can go out and have a few beers together. I would hate to see this side of the game come to an end. It doesn't happen in professional football and, although I'm very much in favour of rugby players being fairly recompensed for the time and effort that an international career costs them, if the social side of the game suffered then that would be a very high cost to pay indeed and it wouldn't be for the betterment of the game as a whole.

The next port of call in my début season was Twickenham. To be honest, in my younger days I was always a bit intimidated going to Twickers. There's just something about the 'Swing Low Sweet Chariot' atmosphere that I didn't like. I came to terms with it over time but when you go down there for the first time to the English HQ it is quite an unsettling experience.

The actual playing surface at Twickenham is a bit odd too. There is a terrific camber on the pitch and when you stand on the middle of the field you can't see the touchlines. Before the game Geech took us out on to the pitch to point this out and to warn us that if we were going to be kicking for touch then to make sure that the ball went into the stands because you were never really sure that you were going to put the ball out.

It wasn't much of a game. John Jeffrey scored a try and Peter Dods kicked a couple of penalty goals and a conversion. We got a 12–12 draw. It's incredibly difficult to win Five Nations games away from home and, I suppose, we were reasonably content with that. This was the famous game where Geoff Cooke, the England manager, referred to us as 'scavengers'. He claimed later that he had meant it as a compliment and that we hadn't allowed them to play the type of game that they wanted. Nevertheless, that wasn't how it was depicted in the press and it wasn't how we read it either. The English never cease to amaze me. They must be the most arrogant nation on earth. I don't think they mean it and I don't even think that they realise they are doing it but they just have this knack for putting people's backs up.

A few days before the game the BBC flew my opposite number Dewi Morris up to Scotland for us to do a film piece for *Grandstand*. He came down to the farm at Rawflat and we did our stuff for the cameras. I have to admit that I thought he was a right cocky bugger. He seemed so full of himself. Once the interviews were over I couldn't wait to get down to Twickenham. I'll do my talking on the pitch, I thought to myself, and I reckon I did too. Morris, who was winning his first Five Nations cap and Rob Andrew didn't have a particularly good game and I reckon that I had the upper hand on Dewi throughout. So my first visit to Twickenham ended with honours even. Morris was dropped by England at the end of the season. Maybe I played just a little part in his temporary downfall. At the press conference afterwards an Irish journalist declared: 'If Cooke thinks that Scotland were a bunch of scavengers just wait until we get hold of the English at Lansdowne Road.'

It's no secret that of all the rugby nations, we don't get on well with England. We're not alone in that. No matter where you go every country will tell you that they want to beat England. In one sense that's a compliment to them but in another it's a dreadful indictment on how the English have conducted themselves over the years.

At the dinner after my first Calcutta Cup match the two sides didn't really mix at all. This is something unique to England. All of the other Five Nations sides — even the French after their own fashion and before their stars nip off to their 'contracted' nightclubs — mix with each other and have a crack after the game. The English don't. The one occasion that I can remember when they did almost ended in bad-tempered fisticuffs. The England flanker Mickey Skinner, always a bit of a buffoon in my opinion, emptied a jug of water over Kenny Milne. He was drenched and most definitely did not see the funny side. Was there a funny side? Ken's brother David, who propped for Scotland in the 1991 World Cup, was also in the company. He was furious and both Milnes really had to bite the bullet. They were all for taking Skinner outside and administering a bloody good hiding. But good Scottish manners prevailed and they just let the matter drop. Later they received letters from the SRU thanking them for their restraint. It was just as well that they had ignored Skinner's provocation because if the Milne boys had pitched in then we would all have been in behind them. No doubt the English players would have joined in too and it would have looked as though World War III had broken out in London's Hilton Hotel.

Ireland were the visitors to Murrayfield for my fourth cap and what a game it turned out to be. It was the one-hundredth match between the two countries and it was an eight-try spectacular. We won 37–21 and Iwan Tukalo scored a hat-trick. We had led 19–6, at one stage but the Irish clawed back the deficit and by half-time we were 19–21 in arrears. In my experience Scotland *v* Ireland games invariably turn out to be superb entertainment for the spectators. We both play much the same kind of rugby. We relish the broken-play situations and we both love getting in amongst the opposition. Fergus Aherne was my immediate opponent. He was a good scrum-half. Standing next to him he looked as if he was just skin and bone but he was nippy with it and you had to have your wits about you around the scrummage, ruck and mauls.

With Geoff Cooke's 'scavengers' comment still fresh in his mind, the late Bob Munro, a super man, who was chairman of Scottish selectors, quipped afterwards: 'Not bad for a pair of scavengers, eh!'

So, with the final game of my first Five Nations championship still to come my international record read won two, lost one, drawn one. France in Paris was next and that was an experience and a half. The senior players in the side had told us that it was an experience we would never forget. And they were right! Right from the outset it was a hoot. The team bus was escorted from the hotel to the Parc des Princes by motorcycle outriders. These guys looked as if they were auditioning for a stunt show. We went right through the centre of Paris at what seemed like 100 miles per hour. Our motorcycle escort rushed ahead stopping oncoming traffic at junctions and waving us through. Woe betide any poor Parisian motorist who got stuck in our path. The police outriders, quite literally, just kicked them out of the way! The boys lapped it up. We were being flung around inside the bus just as if we were on a roller-coaster. By the time we arrived at the ground we were already on a high. At Parc des Princes the bus goes underground and you have to climb a flight of stairs into the changing-room although it is more like a broom cupboard. It's a poky wee place for an international changing-room. That's for the visitors. By contrast, the French, it is rumoured, have palatial changing facilities and a warm-up room of their own.

It's always noticeable at Parc des Princes that when France come out on to the pitch they are dripping with sweat. They've obviously been warming up somewhere and that gives them an immediate advantage. But whenever any of the visiting sides ask if they can go somewhere to warm up the query is always met with Gallic shrugs of the shoulders and the response that, '*Non* it's not possible, such a facility does not exist.' Pull the other one, Pierre!

So far as the game itself went we were hammered 19–3. We just weren't streetwise enough. Craig and I, in our first Five

Nations season, were just boys against men. We had not won in Paris since 1969 but we felt that we had a real chance that year. It's a different breed of player in France, though, and we never stood a chance. I couldn't get over how big and strong their forwards were. Guys like Rodriguez, Garuet, Erbani and Condom just took us apart.

I found myself up against Pierre Berbizier and that 80 minutes in the Parc des Princes cauldron taught me more about international rugby than anything that had gone before. He just took the mickey out of me. He was standing on my toes at the scrums and was pulling my jersey throughout the game. I just hadn't experienced anything like that before. He was cheating but Owen Doyle, the Irish referee, wasn't pulling him up for it so good luck to him. The lessons I learned stood me in good stead for the years to come. I gave Berbizier too much respect and I have to admit now that I was a bit in awe of him. But that happens to all young internationalists. After the game Berbizier walked off without shaking hands with me and he wouldn't swop jerseys. Obviously I hadn't earned his respect. But I never forgot that torrid afternoon and when we went back two years later I gave as good as I got. At the end of that game Berbizier was all over me wanting to shake my hand and congratulate me on a good afternoon's work. We still lost on that second visit to Paris but I felt that I had got the better of Berbizier. The fact that he wanted to talk to me, and we even had a pint together, meant that I had passed the test. I had earned his respect.

In-between those two visits to France we had beaten the French 21–0 in the Grand Slam season game at Murrayfield. When we went back to Paris in 1991 we were really psyched up. The coaches had reminded us how we had been blown away in 1989 and warned us not to allow ourselves to be intimidated as we had been on that occasion. Unfortunately, things got out of hand and fights were breaking out all over the place. We lost 15–9 but we were so psyched up that it probably cost us the game. We lost sight of what it was we were there for, which was to win the game of rugby and not to score more points in the boxing match.

I even got myself into a wee bit of bother with the French full-back and captain Serge Blanco. He was a national hero in France and was winning his world-record eighty-second cap. We had a bit of a scrap and were left lying on the ground knocking lumps out of each other when play had moved away to the other side of the pitch. The sequel came at the dinner after the game when I was nearly accosted by a couple of old Parisian women outside the hotel. They were waving their umbrellas at me and shouting that I was the one who had had a 'go' at Serge. The Frenchmen had been bad enough at the Parc. I didn't fancy taking on their umbrella-wielding womenfolk on the streets of Paris!

That, then, was my introduction to international rugby. I was loving it. In each game I learnt something new and at the end of that season I was chosen to go to Australia with the British Lions. That was a huge bonus so soon in my international career but I was ready to grab the chance with both hands. Next stop the land of Oz.

CHAPTER 4

WALLOPING THE WALLABIES

British Lions in Australia 1989

THE INVITATION to tour with the British Lions in Australia came at the end of the Five Nations tournament. At that time I was a real international novice. I had played only five times for Scotland yet here I was about to embark on the greatest rugby adventure of my life.

I reckon that in a way I was lucky. As I've said elsewhere, your first season in international rugby is often the easiest. Of course you've still got to be able to do the business at international level but, for a scrum-half in particular, you're very much an unknown quantity, still able to spring a surprise or two on the opposition because they're still not tuned into your style of play.

I realised, of course, that with a tour in the offing, all of the Five Nations games were trial games for the Lions. That, though, was always at the back of the mind. The main thing for me was to play well for Scotland and if that meant that a Lions call was likely then, to my mind, that was just a huge bonus.

There were nine Scots on the trip plus Ian McGeechan as coach. Fin Calder was named captain and I was joined by Craig Chalmers, David Sole, Derek White, John Jeffrey, Gavin and Scott Hastings and Peter Dods. That was quite a high Scottish contingent and, with eleven Englishmen, eight Welshmen and four Irishmen, was probably a fair reflection of the Home Unions side's performances in that season's Five Nations Championship.

For Craig and me the fact that we were included represented a dream come true. Chic had come into the Scotland side at the start of the Championship whereas I had won my first cap at Murrayfield against Australia right at the start of the season. We had come a long way in a very short space of time. Not bad for two wee Border boys.

My rivals for the scrum-half berth were Rob Jones of Wales, Fergus Aherne of Ireland and Dewi Morris and Richard Hill of England. I was probably helped by the fact that England hadn't been able to make up their minds whether Morris or Hill was their first-choice scrum-half. I reckoned that I'd had the better of Aherne and deserved to be chosen ahead of him but I knew almost from the start that I would be going as second choice to Jones who at that time was probably the best scrum-half in the world. The fact that, as the tour progressed, we became great mates made it easier for me to accept second billing.

We were to be away for eight weeks and I had never been away from home for such a length of time. Also, it was my first serious rugby tour. It can't be bad to log your first rugby trip abroad with the Lions. But, really, before the selection had been announced I was quite fatalistic about my chances. I was never on tenterhooks waiting for the announcement. When the letter arrived I was chuffed but it wasn't quite the same as getting the note from Murrayfield which informs you that you have won your first cap for your country. That's in a different class altogether.

Almost as soon as the squad was announced we began training. The Scottish complement, working to training schedules produced by Geech and his assistant Roger Uttley, trained throughout the late spring and early summer. We worked out under the eagle eyes of Jim Telfer, Derrick Grant and Dougie Morgan. All of the other nations were supposed to be doing the same but it was noticeable that, the first time we got together as a squad in London, the Scots were a lot fitter than the rest. That has been a feature of Scottish sides over the past decade. We always seem to have the edge on fitness and it has stood us in good stead when the going has got tough.

One of the great things that rugby has to offer is the camaraderie which exists among friend and foe and it was in Australia that I struck up an enduring friendship with Rob Jones, the Welsh scrum-half. We just seemed to get on with each other from day one.

He was going as first choice. He was the more experienced man and was really playing at the top of his form in 1989. He has been in and out of the Welsh side since but, for my money, he was always the best scrum-half in Wales and I just cannot believe that the Welsh selectors could ever have thought otherwise.

However, back in 1989, I had no intention of handing him the Lions' number one spot on a plate. After the first couple of games all of the players have a pretty clear idea as to how the Test side is panning out. But anything can happen and you just have to hang on in there. Paul Dean of Ireland was picked as first-choice fly-half ahead of England's Rob Andrew and our own Craig Chalmers, but Dean lasted half a game and, lo and behold, Andrew was on the next plane out. Craig was dropped and Andrew was in. Anything can happen on tour and you have to be ready.

At the time Rob Jones was the right choice. He was an established player and I was just a novice at international level. I was a wee bit disappointed that I didn't get into the top side for the Anzacs game against a combined Australian/New Zealand side which brought down the curtain on the tour. Rob had played in all of the Tests and I reckoned they might have given that one to me. However, and for whatever reason, they didn't but not making that Test side certainly didn't colour what was a great experience for me.

Australia was a magnificent place to tour even although the Australians themselves were less than welcoming on many occasions. They referred to us throughout as Poms which, as a

Scotsman, really got up my nose. But as soon as they found out that there were indeed some of us who were Scottish, or Irish, or Welsh, then everybody was great. Really, it's just the English that the Aussies are not too keen on. So that's something we have in common!

The first week of the tour was spent in Perth, Western Australia. It was like paradise. The weather was superb, the five-star hotel was even better and the training went like a dream. We were training, golfing, swimming and doing a bit of sightseeing in-between. If this is touring, I thought, then count me in for the duration.

The tour kicked off with a 44–0 win over Western Australia. Rob Jones played in that game and that was the first indication, not that I needed any really, that he was the first-choice scrum-half. In one way it's quite difficult going on tour as a scrum-half because you never really get a chance to relax. You are always either playing or sitting on the bench. So throughout the tour I was either on the side or acting as understudy to Rob. Paul Dean was injured in that game and, sadly for him, he was soon to be homeward bound with Rob Andrew being flown out as his replacement.

After that opener in Western Australia we jetted east to Melbourne where we were to take on Australia 'B'. But it was the 'B' side in name only. They had ten of what was to be their Test side in the line-up and so we knew that we were in for a stern trial. The game was played on a pitch which had been virtually waterlogged by incessant rain. They had tried to do something about it by spreading sand on the turf. The upshot was that we played up to our ankles in glaur. It was just like being back home again.

Rugby in Australia is very physical. I had won my first cap against the Aussies at Murrayfield the year before so I had a fair inkling of what to expect. They set great store by what they consider to be their macho national image and they certainly don't take any prisoners on the rugby field. In fact, on their own patch with Australian referees they seemed to get away with a lot more. You end up having to play the opposition, the refs, the touch-judges, the spectators, the media, the lot. That was my first real experience of how, on a tour, you feel that it is you against the world. You are in an alien country and everything and everybody seems to be against you. That's why team spirit is so important. We were lucky in 1989 in that we all got on so well together and it is this sense of 'family' which really brings you through a tour when it really does feel that everything and everyone outwith your immediate group is conspiring against you.

The game against the supposed Australian shadow side was a tough one. We went behind a couple of times but the guys showed real guts to fight back and we got our noses in front at the finish. We were desperately keen not to let the side down. The first game had been won well and we wanted to continue in a similar vein. It's really important on tour that you keep winning. Nothing succeeds like success and if you can go through a tour with both the Saturday and the midweek sides winning then it serves as a real tonic for morale. Eventually we won 23–18 and it was a real Scottish monopoly on the scoresheet. I got a try, John Jeffrey got two and Gavin Hastings had a conversion and a couple of penalty goals.

As Finlay kept reminding us we were going to be there for eight weeks and that was a long, long time if we started losing. The incentive was always there to keep the heads up by treating every game, no matter where it was or who the opposition was, as an absolute must in terms of the win.

It took me about a fortnight to settle down. I was suffering from dreadful insomnia. My bodyclock had been completely thrown by the 15-hour flight out. I just couldn't get to sleep at night. Whenever we were travelling by bus or flying on to our next port of call I would immediately fall fast asleep. At one point Fin said to me: 'Gary, you're always bloody sleeping. You're like Rip van Winkle.' I don't know whether it was jet lag or whatever but every night for almost a fortnight I would be up wandering around our hotels, totally on my own, at three o'clock in the morning. It took a couple of weeks before my internal time-clock got itself adjusted and after that I was as right as rain.

Next on the agenda was Queensland. It was a Saturday game and once again Rob was in the side. I knew from that point on that he was going to be the number one choice at scrum-half. He was playing well, though, and I had no qualms about not making the top side. That didn't mean that I took a back seat. Far from it. I continued to give my all on the basis that I still wanted to impress the management and also because if Rob had me breathing down his neck then that would spur him on to play even better. That was typical of the spirit within that Lions party. We really were one for all and all for one and that was the spirit which brought us through when things started to get a bit tricky after the first Test.

Even this early on in the proceedings Rob and I had really hit it off. We established a routine of having a few cocktails in the evening before we went for our meal with the rest of the lads. Quite a few times we were the worse for wear before the night was out but when you are on a tour like that, training every day, normal service with regard to hangovers and so on seems to be suspended. Right enough, you don't feel too great at training first thing after a night on the tiles but you soon have all the alcohol sweated out and after training and a good sleep you feel as good as new.

Donal Lenihan was skippering the midweek side. Donal's Doughnuts we were called. Don't ask me why. The crack was great. Donal was a first-class captain and a good player as well. Wherever we were, the Irish boys in the side could be relied upon to track down the Guinness bars. Steve Smith was the great expert. He must have some kind of in-built detection device. It didn't matter where we were, within an hour of arriving he would have established the location of the nearest hostelry which stocked the Irish nectar.

The Saturday side, which by that time was shaping up as the probable Test combination, defeated a very strong Queensland outfit 19–15. It was a hard, physical game and just a taster for what was to come in the Tests. Queensland had gone for 25 games without defeat and they didn't take too kindly to being beaten. Their captain, the Wallaby lock Bill Campbell, was mouthing off a bit at the reception afterwards, saying that he couldn't wait until he met the Lions again in the first Test. By this time, too, the Australian press was beginning to build up a real head of steam about what they claimed was the overly physical nature of the Lions' play. Coming from Aussies that was a bit rich but we took it as a compliment. We reckoned that we had them worried.

I was next on duty against Queensland 'B'. Rob Andrew had just joined the party in place of Paul Dean and he made his début for the Lions in that game. As we now know, he would go on to take Craig's place as first-choice stand-off after the first Test. Obviously at the time that was a big blow to Chic's pride but, looking back, it was probably right that Andrew went in as first choice. Chic was very young and, although he had the footballing ability which he has always possessed, he didn't have the experience that was required in the tense atmosphere of a Lions Test match. Like me, he was a newcomer to international rugby and didn't really have the nous to handle a situation like that.

Having said that, Craig probably played himself into the side for the first Test with his performance against New South Wales. I was on the bench again and watched as the Lions won 23–21. Craig dropped three goals, the final one in the last minute to secure the win.

Donal's Doughnuts played New South Wales 'B' four days later and we survived a bit of a scare, coming back from being 22–11 down at the interval to win 39–19. I got a try but the main thing was that the Wednesday side kept winning. It was important for the morale of the whole party that we did our bit. If the midweek side is winning then that takes a lot of pressure off the boys who are playing in the Saturday games. As things turned out Donal's Doughnuts ended the tour with a clean sheet, the only loss of the entire 12-match trip being in the opening Test.

In retrospect, we were probably over-confident going into the opening Test match at the Sydney football stadium. We had won all of our games, most importantly, winning the Saturday matches against some pretty fierce opposition. We had played against everybody who would be wearing the Wallaby shirt in Sydney and we didn't think that we had too much to worry about.

I was on the bench for the Test and watched horrified as the Australians took us apart. They dominated the lineouts where Steve Cutler and Bill Campbell never let our guys get a sniff of the ball. Nick Farr-Jones and Michael Lynagh controlled the game with ease and, generally, the Lions were well cuffed 30–12.

However, and again with the benefit of hindsight, I reckon it was the best thing that could have happened to us. We were getting too nonchalant. After that defeat in Sydney we knew, if we didn't before, that we weren't there for a holiday. Fin said after the game that the Lions would never play so badly again. And we didn't.

Finlay was under hellish pressure after that Test defeat. The British press, or more particularly the English press, wanted him out. Fin is very much his own man and was well able to cope with all the dirt which came his way but I'm sure that if the captain had been a lesser man then he would have cracked up.

Everybody rallied around and, despite what the media was saying, there wasn't a single person in the tour party who reckoned that Fin should have gone. Another Scottish Lions skipper, Mike Campbell-Lamerton, had dropped himself in Australia in 1966 after the same kind of criticism but there was never any chance that Fin would have followed suit. Even Andy Robinson, the Englishman whom the press wanted to take Fin's place, felt that Calder should stay in the side. The entire team that afternoon were responsible for the defeat, not just one man. There was just no fire about them. The blend didn't seem to be right and before the second Test a week later the management made five changes. Wade Dooley and Mike Teague came into the pack in place of Rob Norster and Derek White, while in the backs Rob Andrew, Scott Hastings and Jerry Guscott replaced Craig, Mike Hall and Brendan Mullin.

But before the Test side could get their revenge, the Doughnuts had to play Australian Capital Territories at the Sieffert Oval, Queanbeyan. ACT were no walkovers. They had beaten a host of touring sides and had recently beaten France and almost achieved victory over the All Blacks too. Before the game the coaches and Finlay told us all how important it was that we got a win. The tour was in grave danger of disintegrating and it was imperative that we got the victory which would keep the Lions on an even keel.

It almost didn't happen. We were 22–11 down at half-time and things were beginning to look pretty bleak. David Sole, who was sitting on the bench, came on midway through the second half as a wing-forward. We pulled it all together in the second period and ran out winners 41–25. I scored my second try of the tour and with that win we shut the critics up and, more importantly for us, we shut the public address up as well. Every time ACT scored they played 'Kookaburras, kookaburras 1–2–3, we are the boys of the ACT'. It really got on my wick. By the end, though, we weren't hearing it quite so often!

The ACT game was also notable for one of the most amazing things I've ever seen on a rugby field. They had a scrum on our 22. It had been their put-in and they won the ball. Nothing extraordinary about that. I had retreated behind our number 8 Derek White to cover the blind-side. Out of the corner of an eye I noticed that the ACT blind side winger was running infield but without the ball. I wondered what the hell was going on. I didn't have long to wait to find out. He got the ball and ran straight up the back of their scrummage and jumped over our scrum. He dropped just in front of me and as he did so he half stumbled. Ten out of ten for artistic content. Zero out of ten for execution. As he fell to the ground we just gave him the most hellish shoeing. The ref awarded a penalty to us for the winger's somewhat unorthodox approach but then he reversed it when we all gave him a touch of the slipper. It was worth it.

The light relief at Queanbeyan over, the second Test loomed on the horizon and we went into it with confidence rebuilt. The pack which the Lions sent out for the Brisbane Test was just awesome. It is certainly the best pack of forwards that I have ever seen. Sole, Moore and Young made up the first row. Ackford and Dooley were the locks and the backrow comprised Calder, Richards and Teague. If the Lions couldn't have won with a pack like that then they were never going to win anything, anywhere.

The Test became known as the Battle of Ballymore. It was never part of the Lions' strategy to resort to dirty play but the coaches had told the Test side that they wanted a physical game in which they were to knock the wind out of the Australians. Mayhem erupted at the first scrummage. Rob Jones had been told that he wasn't to give Farr-Jones an inch. He stood on the Wallaby skipper's toe at the scrummage put-in. Nick shoved Jonesey and it just started from there. Both sides were extremely keyed up and the bout of fisticuffs which erupted was probably the best thing that could have happened. After that, with the exception of a pretty daft bit of stamping by Dai Young, both sides just got on with the rugby. It was hard, physical rugby and the most pathetic thing about it was the way that the Australians started whingeing afterwards.

The Lions won 19–12, the Test series was squared and the show was back on the road. The Australian media went loopy. 'British Lions Thugby Players' was one of the more pleasant headlines. The Australian RFU, too, suffered a brainstorm with threats to send a video of the game to the Home Unions committee back home. As if they were going to do anything about it. They were supposed to be on our side. The whole thing was just a got-up effort to unsettle us for the series decider in a week's time. It didn't work, though. We reckoned that we had the measure of the Aussies and the beer flowed like water on the Saturday night after Ballymore.

By the end of the tour, and this happens on any trip abroad, you really are just ready to go home. After seven weeks in Australia, like everybody else, I just wanted to get home. Living in a suitcase begins to take its toll. Playing Saturdays, travelling Sundays, playing Wednesdays, travelling Thursdays, really takes it out of you. By the end of the seventh week, with the series won, everybody was just looking forward to getting on to the plane which would take us home.

For the duration of a high-profile rugby tour you live your life in a goldfish bowl. You are watched almost every minute of the day. You are watched when you're training, when you're playing, when you're relaxing in the hotel and even when you're walking down the street to the shops. It certainly takes some getting used to. You also know that you are an ambassador for your country and so you have to be on your best behaviour throughout. You can't get 'falling-down' drunk and you have to be polite to the scores of absolute bores who crawl out of the woodwork whenever a rugby touring side is in town. Touring is an experience that I love but it's hard work. People ask how eight weeks in Australia doing something you really enjoy could be hard work but it is. There are so many pressures on the players and management and, frankly, I think the fact that there aren't more 'hotel wrecker' stories, speaks volumes for the way that most rugby folk conduct themselves.

Being the centre of attraction affects different people in different ways. I was a bit disappointed on that tour with the likes of Jeremy Guscott. He was young and, like me, he was just starting out but he got a bit stroppy when kids came up asking for autographs. We would go out to cafés for coffee and sticky buns and would always be pestered by autograph hunters. I didn't mind because I suppose when I was a kid I would have done the same thing myself. However, Jerry used to get really upset when the autograph hunters gathered around, so much so that Fin had a word with him to the effect that no matter how tiresome it was, it was best to be polite at all times.

After the second Test we had a week off. The entire party jetted off to Cairns away up in the north-east just to recharge the batteries. That was a tremendous week. We went skin-diving and snorkelling and generally just did the tourist bit. We also put in some hard training stints and the two combined were the perfect preparation for the series decider back down in Sydney.

We were confident going into the third Test. Against all the predictions, there was none of the brawling which had featured in the earlier games. Ieuan Evans sneaked a try off David Campese and, unfortunately for Campo, that was the turning-point of the game and the series. He threw out a pretty stupid pass to the Wallaby full-back Greg Martin. It would have been bad enough if it had happened inside our 22 but Campese chose his own in-goal area in which to have his brainstorm. Martin dropped the ball and Evans pounced for the try. Campese is a brilliant player who does a lot of wonderful things but he cocked up in spades that afternoon in Sydney. Throughout his career he has done things that nobody else would ever have attempted. Sometimes they work and sometimes they don't. That one, though, was about as big a blunder as I've ever seen on a rugby field. I have to admit that I felt sorry for him because maybe his mistake cost Australia the series. I say maybe because, in my book, the Lions were going to win anyway. Nevertheless, Campese will take the memory of that goal-line blunder to his grave.

The Lions won 19–18 and, probably, the scoreline flattered the Wallabies. The scenes in the dressing-room afterwards were unbelievable, The 'tinnies' got big licks and that was just the start for an evening of marvellous liquid entertainment. When we got back to the hotel Rob Jones and I were first into the bar as usual. The cocktails were flowing that night, I can tell you. Even after seven weeks we still didn't know what they were called. The barman just gave us the brochure with all the pictures in it. We just pointed to the picture and the barman made them up to order. They proved to be my undoing one night when, still glowing from an evening in the bar, I decided to phone home. My mother and father were out in Australia so I called brother Kevin. The crack was good but it cost me £78. When I told Shona, who was in the middle of making the final preparations for our wedding, she said: 'You Armstrongs! Blood is thicker than water. You never spend £78 on a phone call to me!'

Say cheese: Me, aged four.

Jed Thistle: and it's seven-a-side success at Riverside Park.

We moved from the Borders to Dunfermline when I was in my teens. Here I am, front row extreme right, with the Dunfermline HS 1st XV.

The semi-junior side Jed Thistle was where I did my growing-up. I'm in the front row, second from the right.

And here I am modelling a new line in headgear: bruising Border League action from 1987, Jed-Forest v Gala.

The Scotland Under-21 side which played Wales in 1987. I'm in the front row, third from the left. Brother Kevin, who was on the bench, is on the extreme left in the back row.

My first Scotland 'B' Cap, against Italy at Aberdeen in 1987. The side was captained by Andrew Ker.

Tense moments before my International debut against Australia at Murrayfield in 1988. My stand-off was the Harlequin Richard Cramb who is sitting on my left.

Was it something I said? Nick Farr-Jones bellows a warning to his pack as I break from a scrum. The year was 1988 at Murrayfield and the occasion was my Scotland debut against Australia.

Another shot from my first Cap game against Australia in 1988. I seem to have got the better of Aussie full-back Andy Leeds.

To the victor the spoils: Jed-Forest win Hawick Sevens in 1989. One of my remaining rugby ambitions is to do the same thing at our own tournament at Riverside Park.

Codes. What codes? Chris Gray seems as confused as I was with the lineout calls in the 1990 Grand Slam game against England.

Armstrong for the high-jump: panic stations against England in 1990.
But all was well that ended well.

Eyes on the ball: Fin Calder, Chris Gray and I all have the same intention. Murrayfield, 1990.

You can tell that we're chuffed: Grand Slam dressing-room joy. Geech, JJ, Chic, Tooks, Chris Gray, Tony Stanger, Fin, me, Scott, Paul Burnell, Gav and Del Boy savour our moment of glory.

Come back: that's, indeed, what Martin Johnson seems to be saying as I make my comeback for Scotland against England in 1994.

The second game during my International comeback season in 1994 was against Ireland in Dublin. Sadly, I damaged a thumb and was sidelined again.

I had one more outing, against a New South Wales Country XV, before it was time to come home. I scored a couple of tries and we won 72–13 which, I think, gives a good impression about the strength of the opposition. Then, there was just the game against the Anzacs to come. Fin stepped down so that Andy Robinson could get a game and, as I've said, I thought that maybe the management would have given me a run instead of Rob but they didn't. Rob was even going to feign injury so that I could come on but we decided against that. That game was won by the margin of 19–15 and so our record of just having lost the one game, albeit the first Test, was kept intact.

Winning tours are invariably successful tours but I don't think there's any doubt that this was a particularly enjoyable trip. The management, the coaching, the captaincy and the playing personnel just came together perfectly. The manager, Clive Rowlands, who in addition to being an internationalist in his own right is also Rob Jones' father-in-law, was first-class. Ian McGeechan underlined his position as the world's best rugby coach and he was ably assisted by Roger Uttley. Fin Calder was just great as captain. He weathered the most monumental of storms and came out smelling of roses at the other end. The touring party itself, in general, was a great bunch of blokes.

Having said all that, though, I was glad to get home. Probably we all were. Eight weeks is a long time to be away. By the end you just long for a bit of privacy. Australia in 1989 was my first experience of touring and I'll say this for it, I don't think that I've ever been so fit as I was when I came back from Down Under. Training every day and eating the best of grub for two months makes you feel like a million dollars. I put on nearly a stone in weight but it was pure muscle.

Six weeks after our return to the UK Shona and I were married. One of the best things about being away in Australia was that Shona had to make most of the arrangements herself — only joking Shona! The wedding, in Jedburgh, served as a reunion for a lot of the Scottish Lions plus the honorary Scot Rob Jones. Rob and wife Megan came north for the wedding and the Scottish press had a bit of a field day. My old Scotland rival Greig Oliver was a guest as well so, almost like Hugh Grant's hit film, it was a case of three scrum-halves and a wedding.

All of the Scots who took part on that tour came back better players. In particular Craig and I really grew up in Australia We knew that we were just as good, if not better, than some of our Lions team-mates and the proof of that particular pudding would be displayed in the very next season when we embarked upon our Five Nations Grand Slam campaign.

CHAPTER 5

CODENAME FIJI

Grand Slam 1990

SATURDAY, 17 MARCH 1990, is one of those dates that's engraved in my mind like it was put there with a hammer and chisel. Grand Slam Saturday. The best day of my rugby life. It was the day of the underdog and it was the day that we beat the odds-on favourites for one of the biggest prizes that rugby can offer.

It was also the day — and I've never breathed a word of this until now — that Armstrong flew by the seat of his pants and did so to such convincing effect that no one had the slightest notion that anything was amiss. My team-mates never knew. The 55,000-strong Murrayfield crowd never knew. And the millions watching the match on worldwide television didn't know either. All will be revealed later. But first, let's take a look at the campaign which put us in the unique position of taking on England in a winner-takes-all game in which the Calcutta Cup, Triple Crown, Championship and Grand Slam were all there for the taking. At the time of writing it's been five years since that glorious season but — with only three Grand Slams in the history of Scottish rugby — I reckon that maybe I can be excused a wallow in the rosy glow of nostalgia.

At the start of the season we had a couple of pre-Christmas outings, both at home, against Fiji and Romania. Both were won pretty convincingly but perhaps more significantly we had a new captain. David Sole had taken over from Fin Calder for the game against Fiji and the appointment of the ruthless and enigmatic Sole turned out to be an inspired choice. I was winning my sixth cap against Fiji and so I was in that strange position of being no longer a 'new boy' while at the same time not being a permanent fixture in the side. I was, though, beginning to feel more at ease in a Scotland jersey. I had played through the previous Five Nations Championship and had appeared against Australia at the beginning of the 1988–89 season, so as far as the opposition was concerned, I was becoming something of a known quantity.

I was settling into the side and coming to terms with the much harder questions that international rugby asks of those who take part. There really is no way you can prepare for the huge step-up from club or district rugby to the altogether tougher scenario of a fully fledged international match. The only preparation for international rugby is international rugby itelf. Nevertheless, I've always reckoned that it's easy — relatively speaking — during your first season of international rugby. And this is especially the case in my position. In your first season you don't appear on rival coaches' tactical videos. You're a stranger and the opposition don't really know how you play. Because you're new on the scene and you don't appear on videotape the opposition can't lock on to your style of play. You can just play your natural game and never mind the consequences. But once you've been around for a season then the opposition have you taped. Literally. All coaches now make such full and profitable use of video recordings that every aspect of your next opponent's game is studied and analysed in the most minute detail. Most international coaches now have their own mini-editing studios where they can cut and trim sequences from a game to use in their next coaching sessions. There are few, if any, secrets in international rugby.

I certainly found that my second season with Scotland was much harder than the first. Once the opposition have analysed your strengths and weaknesses and pin-pointed your favourite plays then they make their counter-plans which are intended to nullify your influence on the game. In fact I would go further and say that with every season that passes international rugby gets more, not less, difficult. No matter how many caps you've got you still have to impress the selectors and, although you could be excused for doubting it with regard to some recent Scottish performances and the play of a few veteran players, you are still only as good as your last game.

When I was injured and Andy Nicol came into the side for the 1992 Championship season many observers thought that he was a revelation and some even considered that they had unearthed a truly world-class player. I don't mean to be unkind about Andy — who is undoubtedly a fine player — but maybe some of the 'world-class' claims were just a bit premature.

Bearing in mind what I've just said about an international scrum-half's first season being the easiest, it might have been better to have waited a while before saddling Andy with that 'world-class' tag.

Comparisons were obviously made between my style of play and Andy's when he took over when I was injured. I don't think, though, that my style of play can be categorised really. I do a bit of everything. I kick and break and pass. The main thing in an international match, in any game really, is to establish the link with your stand-off. If that link is operating smoothly, like a well-oiled hinge, then the whole team ticks. You have to break now and again and you have to vary your game. You have to keep the opposition guessing. I just try to keep the other team thinking all the time. You have to get them into two minds. They should never be able to predict what you are going to do next. If you try to link with your stand-off all the time, which is what the purists want, then sooner or later they'll catch up with your stand-off. The golden rule is never, ever to dish out bad ball. I was re-watching a tape of the Grand Slam game against England and an incident summed up my philosophy. A move had been called and the ball was supposed to go quickly to Gavin. But I caught a brief glimpse of a couple of English defenders just on the periphery of my vision and I held the ball back. I would rather take a beating than give somebody else a hospital pass when the opposition have got five or six yards to get up a head of steam and really give him a going over.

It can be coached, especially if you're caught at a young age. Mostly, though, it's instinct. You can feel the gap. There's really no other way to describe it. You really do feel the space. You have got to be completely aware, though. A lot of folk reckon that I was like a third wing-forward, setting up ball and so on, but I think to be a top scrum-half in today's game you have to be willing to mix it with the forwards. You're the closest back to the opposing pack and it's often your responsibility to take the ball over the gain line. The gain line is the magic borderline between success and failure. If you can get over the gain line then you keep your forwards going forward. There's nothing worse for your pack than for them to have to turn and play in retreat. You should always keep your big men going full steam ahead. If you can achieve that on a regular basis then the backs have a platform to work off and that was something that the 1990 Grand Slam side had honed to perfection.

The first game of the Grand Slam season was against Fiji. These particular South Sea islanders have been very much eclipsed by the Western Samoans, especially since the 1991 World Cup, but back at the tail end of 1989 they were still to be taken seriously. They were big, strong men who could handle and who were as dangerous as anybody when they had the ball in their hands and a bit of space in which to work. I didn't know much about them, I had never heard of my opposite number but then I never cared much who I was playing against. My first objective was always to follow Roy Laidlaw's advice and to get the link with my stand-off operating smoothly. Achieve that and everything else would follow. We controlled the game throughout and won 38–17, running in six tries including two from new boy Tony Stanger. And what a début season he was going to have.

Six weeks later the Romanians visited Murrayfield and we exerted total control to beat them 32–0. Tony Stanger got a hat-trick and Fin Calder was back in the side after a well-earned break during which he had recharged his batteries after the gruelling Lions tour to Australia that summer. It's worth mentioning here that it's surely no coincidence that Scotland's three Grand Slams, in 1925, 1984 and 1990, have followed hard on the heels of a Lions tour. Each time the Scots in the touring party have returned to these shores to play out of their skins in the Five Nations Championship. The reason, I'm sure, is that we had seen the lads from the other home countries at close quarters. We had lived cheek by jowl with them for the duration of the tour and we knew that we were just as good as they were. Additionally, in 1990 our coach Ian McGeechan had been the successful Lions coach in Australia and he, therefore, knew the strengths and weaknesses of our Five Nations opponents better than they knew them themselves.

In the New Year, then, we were in our starting blocks for the Five Nations campaign with two satisfying wins already under our belts. We also had a settled team and a group of individuals who knew each other inside out. We used only 16 players throughout the championship season — and then only because Derek Turnbull substituted for the injured Derek White in the final game — and by the end we were playing almost like a club side.

By the time we made our entrance into the Championship against the Irish at Lansdowne Road it was already two weeks old. A feature of the entire season was that we met every side on the rebound against England, who had demolished the opposition with some first-class performances.

That opening game certainly didn't signal that it was going to be a vintage season. We played badly. OK, we won 13–10 but it was by no means a convincing performance. Geech had been laid low with flu and so Jim Telfer was in charge as we flew on a storm-delayed flight to Dublin. We were fortunate in the quality of the coaches we had throughout that season. Ian was in overall charge but helping him were Jim Telfer, Derrick Grant and Dougie Morgan. These four guys have forgotten more about rugby than most of us will ever know.

'Creamie' Telfer really laid on the patriotism bit in his team talk before we left the Westbury Hotel in the centre of Dublin for the ground just ten minutes' drive away. He got us all together in the team room before we got on to the bus. He had us joining hands in a huddle before going into 'psyching' overdrive. He told us that we were representing ourselves and our families and our country. Then he had us sing *Flower of Scotland*. By the time we got on to the bus supposedly big, hard rugby players were sniffling and wiping the tears from their eyes. Telfer's big message — and he's right — is that it's not enough to play for Scotland. Lots of people have played for Scotland and most people will never remember their names. Winning for Scotland, he says, is the thing that sets apart all of those who have pulled on the dark blue jersey from those who have really deserved their places.

That kind of thing really gets to me. Even now when I watch the TV videos of the games we played that season the tears well in my eyes. That was some team and it really was a privilege to be part of it all.

When we arrived at the ground we were really hyped up but then it all went flat. Nothing worked for us. Craig and I didn't have a great game, the wind was dreadful and the Irish were all over us in the lineout. The Irish played well but we made a lot of unforced errors and if it hadn't been for two tries by Derek White then it would just have been another also-ran of a season.

For the first try, Sean Lineen took the ball on the burst and straightened everything up. He 'popped' to JJ and Derek was at his shoulder to receive the scoring pass. The second one was just off the back of a scrum. It was supposed to have been a set back-row move but Derek broke the Irish tackle and he got in himself, just. The ball was supposed to come out to me with Tony on the outside but you take your chances as they're presented and when Derek broke the tackle the rest of the planned move wasn't necessary.

We had been 7–0 down at half-time, and, apart from the two tries, nothing seemed to go right. We kicked badly and we played badly in the lineout. It was just one of those days when the rub of the green is against you. But we had won despite that and this is the mark of a good side — one which can get a positive result even when they know that they've played well below expectation. In the dressing-room afterwards you would have thought that we had lost. Amid all the gloom the SRU president Jimmy McNeil actually thought that we had! However, it had been a win away from home and it gave us something to build on. We had two weeks in which to make our preparations for the French at Murrayfield and the coaches used the time wisely and profitably. We really tightened up on our lineout work and were much better prepared by the time that the French match came around.

France had not won at Murrayfield since 1978, so impressive had Scotland's home record become, that the ground was dubbed Fortress Murrayfield. We went on to the field expecting to win but had to make sure, also, that we didn't underestimate the Frenchmen. They had suffered a humiliating 26–7 defeat at the hands of the English in Paris and were desperate to make amends for that. We eventually beat them 21–0 but the scoreline doesn't tell the whole story. It was a much closer game than that. We led by just 3–0 at half-time and really, it was only after the Frenchman Alain Carminati was sent off by Fred Howard for stamping on JJ's head that we took control. The French are a queer side to play against. They are far more physical than any of the other Northern Hemisphere teams. Also, their mental attitude is different. Frankly, there's a touch of the psycho about them. They go in for a win-at-all-costs style and they always seem to have at least a couple of real nutters in their team.

They proved it again that day with Carminati. He made absolutely no effort to hide the fact that he was stamping on JJ's head. He could have done any amount of damage. Or, come to think of it, maybe not!! There was no doubt, though, that he deserved to go. John was probably holding on to the Frenchman's foot and he just lost the rag. They have a real problem with temperament. If you get at them then they begin to lose their cool.

When the game isn't going their way then the French start to yap at each other. That's when you know you've got them. They just went to pieces after Carminati went off and the game became just like all the others I've played against them. You have to be so streetwise because they're the biggest bunch of cheats that I've ever played against. They'll try absolutely anything to get the game going in their favour. There's more jersey pulling and more fly digs in the ribs against the French than in the rest of the season put together. You just have to try and ignore them.

Henri Sanz of Narbonne, who was my immediate opponent that day, was playing his first Five Nations game. He was quite a cocky wee bugger. Pierre Berbizier had been dropped to make way for him but he didn't get many caps after that. He was up to the usual shoving and pushing and toe-stamping at the scrummage put-in. Good luck to him. He had come to stamp his authority on the game and it was up to me to make sure that he didn't win the psychological battle and I don't think he did. You have to earn your respect in international rugby.

So, it was mission accomplished, two down and two still to go. It had been a better performance against the French but nobody was talking about a Grand Slam at this stage. We were looking forward to taking on the Welsh in Cardiff and we were sure that we would be in a better frame of mind than we had been when we had travelled to Dublin. The coaches kept everything low-key and we just took one game at a time.

It's probably worth talking a bit here at the midway point in the campaign about the make-up of the team and in particular the captain and his lieutenants. As I've already said, David Sole had taken over from Fin Calder as skipper at the start of the season. Sole was a superb captain. His attitude was absolutely brilliant. He never left you in any doubt as to what it was he wanted. He wasn't a man who said a lot but every word counted. He was also a ruthless competitor. He hated being beaten and he led by example. People who don't know what they're talking about speak about 'putting your body on the line' and sometimes that's exactly what it's about. You can get hurt badly.

But with David that's just what he did. I never saw him flinch. He was incredibly brave and the rest of the guys tried to follow his example.

Over and above that he was a superbly gifted rugby player. He could do things that no prop forward should ever have been able to do. His handling was superb and his speed over that first 20 metres was just unbelievable. He was regularly the fastest guy in the entire Scotland squad when it came to 50-metre sprints. Soley really liked to get involved. He was a prop who played like a back-row forward. They reckon he wasn't that great a scrummager when he first started in the international side but by the time that I came along he had really worked at that aspect of his game and he never let Scotland down.

Additionally, when he played for the Lions in Australia in 1989 I think he was probably the best prop in the world. He more than held his own in the scrummage but, in the rest of his play, he brought a new dimension to what a prop is supposed to be able to do. With lots of props you never heard their name mentioned but Soley was into everything. He was always at the heart of the action.

He wasn't somebody who shouted and swore and got excited. At team talks he spoke very softly but in a scary kind of way. His eyes were incredible. They just stared right through you. I wouldn't have liked to play against him in an international side because he was just so ruthlessly committed that it sent shivers down your spine. David would be the first to admit that he was aided and abetted throughout that season by Jeffrey and Calder. Those two plus Gavin and Scott Hastings would meet with David away from the rest of the team and they would work out their strategies.

Off the field Sole was a bit of a solitary figure. He was a very deep character who kept himself very much to himself. Even when you were chatting to him you never knew whether you were really getting through to him or not. Not many of us really got to know him but as a skipper we would have followed him anywhere. He was a great contradiction. Off the field he was this quiet, almost shy guy who kept his thoughts to himself. But on the rugby field he was a bit of an animal. He did whatever had to be done and he never shirked anything. Finlay and JJ were the same. They were absolutely ruthless and never took a backward step. They were never 'feart' to put their bodies on the line for the good of the team and that's what makes a good team a great team — when every single one of you will go just that bit further for the good of the team as a whole.

Fin and JJ helped David through the rough patches, and there were rough patches particularly later when the issue of commercialism began to make an impact. David acted as the players' representative when negotiating with potential sponsors and I don't think that this went down well with certain folk at Murrayfield. However, in a playing sense, David had a great relationship with the coaches. He was particularly close to Geech and they just made up a superb team.

That, then, was the High Command which led us through the Grand Slam campaign and next in the firing line were Wales. They had gone through a bad patch and were in some disarray. John Ryan had resigned as coach after his side had lost heavily 34–6 to England. The Welsh nation almost went into mourning as their rugby heroes were shown to be human after all. Ron Waldron of the highly successful Neath club was the man chosen to lead Welsh rugby to the Promised Land. Sadly for him, though, it turned out to be a land full of broken promises. With Waldron installed as national coach he picked seven Neath men for his coaching début against us but he was soon to discover that what had worked on the club scene in Wales didn't translate so well to the international arena. The Neath front row were selected en masse. Unfortunately for Wales, they weren't in the same league as the Pontypool front row of fame and legend which had served the Principality so well in the Seventies.

That Neath front row was an odd bunch. They all had close-cropped hair and they looked like a bunch of convicts. Sometimes they acted on the pitch like that as well. At the dinner after the game I was sitting at the same table as Brian Williams, the loosehead prop. It was incredible. He never used his knife and fork once. I don't know who he was trying to impress or whether he was trying to live up to the wild-men image which he and his Neath colleagues were fostering but, frankly, he was just pathetic. It was sheer ignorance. He ate every scrap of food with his bare hands. I don't know if this was what passed for normal in the Williams household but it struck me as being 'gey weird' behaviour at an international rugby black-tie banquet.

Williams and his front-row partners Kevin Phillips and John Pugh more than lived up to their skinhead image on the park as well. They were mental. They were small and light for an international front row and, frankly, they were scrummaged off the park, but in the loose they were a real handful. We had to watch out for the quick, tap penalties which were a Neath trademark and, as I recall, it was from just such a move that we were caught unawares and they scored their only try of the afternoon.

For me, the trip to Wales provided an opportunity to meet up again with Robert Jones, my old mate from the 1989 Lions tour in Australia. We had really hit it off and began a close friendship which lasts to this day. I really felt for Rob, as he was captaining the Welsh side and they were going through such a dreadful period. In love, war and international rugby, though, anything goes and feelings of friendship were set aside for the 80 minutes of the game. There was, however, one incident for which I was blamed and in which — on this occasion at least — I was an entirely innocent party. We were defending a scrummage near our own line. Kenny Milne took an unexpected strike against the head and those in the know reckoned that as Robert had settled himself to put the ball into the tunnel, I had knocked it from his hands and straight into our side of the scrum. On this occasion I plead not guilty. It was a tactic I had used often enough in the past when the referee's attention was distracted — in fact we used to con the referee into moving around to the other side of the scrummage when Sole would make out that there was trouble brewing between himself and his opposite number — but on this occasion it wasn't me. I admit that I was just about to do it and got myself ready to nudge the ball out of Robert's hands and into the scrum when our tight-head prop Paul Burnell beat me to it.

He flicked his right boot up and took the ball clean out of Rob's hands. On that one occasion at least my conscience is clear. By the end of the Grand Slam season the ploy had more or less run its course. In the decider game against England I tried it out with Richard Hill. Sole collapsed a scrum and David Bishop, the New Zealand referee, went round to the other side to see what was going on but the English boys told him to watch out for me. I nudged the ball in, regardless, but the ref was forewarned and I was promptly penalised for my efforts. It fooled the normally superbly astute Bill McLaren, though. On the BBC video commentary Bill sees the ref having a word with me and declares that he just can't understand what the penalty was for. Well, Bill, now you know!

We didn't play well that afternoon in Cardiff. There was a lot of pressure on us because, obviously, we knew that if we won then we would have England at home for the Grand Slam. Once again, though, we didn't play to our own growing expectations. But we won and that's the sign of a good team. If you can still get a result even when you don't play as well as you know you can then you really are getting somewhere.

The game lacked any kind of continuity. We scored from a lineout. The ball was knocked back as scrap and I took it up the front. I popped it up to Soley and JJ had a bit of a run before Damian Cronin eventually ended up with the ball in his hands and scored in the corner. We led 10–3 at half-time through Damian's try and a couple of penalty goals by Chic. Paul Thorburn kicked a penalty for Wales to keep them in the hunt. In the second half we were getting used to the continual mad rushes by the Neath front row and were quite happy for them to play that way all afternoon. Wales showed what they could have done if they had played it wider when Arthur Emyr went over for a superb try which Thorburn converted. But we kept our noses in front with another penalty from Chic and it ended 13–9 in our favour. They ran us close but I'm sure that the so-called Neath experiment set Wales back. That afternoon the Welshmen — and especially those from Neath — were on an adrenalin high. Some of them were playing like they were from another planet. You can't play international rugby like that. You need a cool head and Wales didn't have one. Truthfully, a lot of the blokes playing for Wales that afternoon didn't deserve to be playing international rugby. They just weren't good enough. They might have been superb club players. They might even have made superb 'B' caps but they weren't good enough to make the huge jump into the full international side.

Ron Waldron himself was a bit of a hard nut. At the dinner after the game, as Williams was scoffing his roast beef in caveman style, Waldron walked past and fixed me with what I took to be an attempt at an intimidating stare.

He said: 'We'll see you next time, pal.' I was quite taken aback. I've always played my rugby hard — even against pals like Robert Jones — and then let bygones be bygones in the bar afterwards. You can relax with a pint and enjoy a 'crack' with the enemy of only a few hours beforehand. But Waldron seemed to be serious. It took place so suddenly and unexpectedly that I couldn't be sure but I'm almost certain that he was issuing some kind of a threat. I just laughed but Waldron wasn't smiling. He didn't last long as Welsh coach. Good riddance I say.

Earlier, the real spirit of the game had been seen when Jonesey and I, Tony Clement, Craig Chalmers and JJ nipped off to The Bank, a huge Cardiff pub, before going on to the official banquet. The welcome we all got from the punters in the place was superb. That, to me, epitomises what rugby is all about and that's the side of Welsh rugby that I choose to remember rather than the sad, almost psychopathic attitude adopted by Waldron and his Neath disciples.

The Grand Slam was now a distinct possibility. We had England at Murrayfield and for the next two weeks we were utterly focused on what lay ahead.

The fortnight between Cardiff and Murrayfield was nerve-racking in the extreme. We would rather have been back in action immediately. But we weren't idle during the time we had on our hands and, in some ways, it worked to our advantage. The time allowed us and the coaches to further hone our play. The management team thought it essential that the squad be kept together so we maintained our regular sessions and, on the Championship weekend which we had to sit out, we were taken to St Andrews where we spent the time doing a bit of training but, in the main, just relaxing. We wanted to keep everything rolling along. That team was so close it was unbelievable. As I've said before, we knew each other so well that we were like a club side.

Once it become clear that our final game against England was to be the great showdown for the Slam and the Championship and all the rest then the media hype really began. We were used to taking calls from the Scottish press but because of the crucial nature of the match we began to get press calls from all over the place. My telephone was red-hot. Ian McGeechan and the manager Duncie Paterson declared that only they and senior players — Sole, Calder, Hastings, Jeffrey — would speak to the media. This kept the press off our backs and it meant that the Scottish camp would all be sending out the same message. From very early on that message was that England were world-beaters and, really, Scotland were just grateful to be allowed to share the field with them.

Geech had reckoned that one factor which might prove to be crucial in England's downfall was over-confidence. So throughout the fortnight leading up to Grand Slam Saturday itself we just went along with all of the hype that was coming from south of the Border. I know that some Scottish rugby fans couldn't believe some of the things that they were reading in the papers. My mates were saying to me: 'What the hell is Sole saying that for,' or 'Did you see what Calder said in the papers today?' but it was all part of the plan. We knew we had the beating of the English. We just didn't tell them that.

It was a time of great tension but here, I think, is where work helps and this is one of the factors that would be missing if top players became full-time professionals. Maybe it wouldn't work for everybody but I was able to escape the pressures of rugby when I was working. I was driving a lorry at the time and found that when I was behind the wheel, even when it was on the cab radio, I could get away from everything but the job in hand.

The actual week leading up to the game was absolutely incredible. I've never experienced anything like it and I don't think the game of rugby has either. In fact, I don't think it will ever happen quite like that again. The media exposure that single game got far exceeded anything that I've experienced with the Lions or during the World Cup in 1991. It seemed like the whole nation was talking about it and everybody was focused on Saturday, 17 March.

We got down to serious business on the Wednesday before the game when the forwards and the half-backs gathered at the Braid Hills Hotel in Edinburgh. We felt that this was it. We were together and wouldn't be apart again until we had played our own wee parts in history and by the time we set off back home we would know whether we had become just the third Scottish side to win a Grand Slam.

The training sessions in the lead-up to that game were the most concentrated that I've ever taken part in. Geech and Jim Telfer, plus Dougie Morgan and Derrick Grant, really put us through our paces and, to my mind anyway, the sessions went perfectly. We had nothing to worry about. The coaches had done their homework well and had pored for hours and hours over videotapes of England. They reckoned that if we could hold them in the scrummage and disrupt them on the touchline — where Dooley and Ackford had played some great rugby — then we would be quids in. Geech knew their play inside out because he had coached them with the Lions in Australia the year before. The forwards really worked on their scrummaging in the sessions before the game and we had no worries in that department. We reckoned that Sole, Milne and Burnell could more than hold their own with Rendall, Moore and Probyn. The lineout, though, was the key. We knew that we had to cancel the advantage which Dooley and Ackford might give England.

The coaches devised a system which was intended to keep the English forwards guessing. Our jumpers moved up and down the line and sometimes we would have Calder, and even David Sole, stationed at the front. Unfortunately, and now — as they say — it can be revealed. It kept me guessing as well.

David Sole and the coaches dreamt up a four-number system of codes and then further complicated it by making the numbers mean something else depending on which 'quarter' of the field we were in at the time. In addition, there were letter codes which would determine whether the ball would be 'off the top' and coming back to me immediately or whether it was going to be held and driven. We also had 'colour' codes for set lineout plays with shortened lines and so on. David would have killed me if he'd known at the time but there were so many codes that I just couldn't remember them all.

Before the game I would be sitting in our hotel with the forwards and Geech would be shouting out codes and asking this and that forward where the ball was going. I used to sit with my head down hoping like hell that he didn't ask me. It was like being back at school! I knew the colour codes and the code for the long-ball over the top but that was about it. For the others I just used to stand on the five-metre line and then work my way back. I would watch where Kenny Milne was throwing the ball and then work my way back to receive it from the forwards. I do the same with Jed. It doesn't bother me and, until now, nobody has known. But I've never much bothered with all this code business and it doesn't seem to have done me any harm.

It's particularly difficult at scrum-half because you're supposed to know all the forward codes plus the codes for the backs and all the penalty move codes and so on. Additionally, with Fin and JJ and Derek White in the side a lot of our plays were built up around them and, at one stage, we had something like 20 back-row moves to remember. Sometimes you felt like a bloody number cruncher. I used to worry about the penalty moves because that was an area where I was central to the action and so I had to make a big effort to remember all the penalty ploys. I couldn't take everything on board and so I used to concentrate mostly on those. But even then I sometimes got it wrong.

Most of those who attend international matches at Murrayfield won't really have a clue about how technical the game has become and that because defences are now so 'professional' there is little room any more for the inspired 'off the cuff' play. That's why there are so many set moves but it makes for a whole lot of learning.

But now the countdown to the Big Day was well and truly on. The squad was pretty relaxed and I did my usual bit to make it more so! I'm one of those guys who just can't sit still. I always have to be up and about, occupying myself with something. If I've got nothing to do in the lead-up to a big game then the chances are that I begin to fret. Inevitably on international weekends this meant mischief!

I suppose really it was just nervous tension but I was the pest of the party — silly things like pinching the television remote controls from the boys' rooms and, more spectacularly, emptying several sachets of hot chocolate powder into Scott Hastings' bath. We had returned to the hotel from a training session and Scott was soaking in a steaming tub. While we chatted I tipped the powder into the water behind his back. I was out of the room and halfway down the corridor when I heard the satisfying result of my work: 'Armstrong, you little bastard. I'll see you later.' He didn't, but for a couple of seasons after that folk used to hide the hot chocolate in their hotel rooms just in case of a repeat performance. Looking back, I suppose it was pretty childish but pranks like these acted as a safety valve for the tension that builds up in the camp during the hours leading up to an international match.

The Friday night before the game is always the worst. On the eve of Grand Slam Saturday Craig Chalmers and I played pool until about 11.30 then we had our hot chocolate — in mugs this time, not the bath — and were tucked up by midnight. Some folk just can't get to sleep on the night before an international and quite often the doc will give them a sleeping tablet. The hot chocolate and a sticky bun always did the trick for me. On the night before the Grand Slam match I was sharing a room with Derek White and he — like Fin Calder — was one of those who always took a couple of whiskies before nodding off to sleep.

The international morning breakfast was always the same for me. It became a bit of a ritual in which Craig would invariably join me — two bacon rolls and lashings of tomato sauce. No doubt the dieticians and all the other experts who're now attached to the Scotland team would throw up their hands in horror but rolls and bacon always set me up well for the rigours of the day.

On Grand Slam morning the backs and the forwards split up and the forwards did some lineout drills on the hotel lawn. I went with the backs! Even as this is written I'm thinking about the bollocking that Jim Telfer is going to give me — even five years later — for not knowing the lineout codes. It couldn't have been that bad, Jim. We won.

After the workout it was brunch, which for me meant a couple of bananas for energy. Before we left the hotel Ian McGeechan gathered us all together for the final team talk. And it was a beauty. Geech really stoked the fires of nationalism. He told us about the letters he'd received from Scots all over the world. He said that Scots all over the globe would be thinking about the one patch of grass that was Murrayfield and that we were playing not only for ourselves, for our families and each other but for all Scots, no matter where they were. He said that his dad had been in the army and that despite the fact that he had stayed all over the place as a youngster, he had never forgotten that he was Scottish, and proud of it. Geech struck just the right note. When he had finished nobody said a word. It soothed the nerves and had made us focus even harder on what we had to do. Nevertheless, it was a real tear-jerker and there were quite a few players with tears in their eyes by the time we clambered on the bus to take us to the ground.

I always found the drive to the stadium the most nerve-racking part of an international weekend. Once you were on the bus then there was no escape. You were on your way; there was no turning back and the countdown to kick-off took on a life of its own. It gets better with experience but even for seasoned internationalists the hour or so before kick-off is very definitely not for those of a nervous disposition.

As soon as we got off the bus at Murrayfield we all sensed that this was something special. As we made our way to the dressing-room through two lines of spectators they started cheering. And that was before the game had even begun. We dumped the gear in our changing-room and then strolled out on to the pitch. The stadium itself was still filling up but there, on our pitch, were the English strolling around as if they owned the place. The BBC were doing interviews with them and their wives. Their wives for goodness sake! It was just too much for the Scots boys to take. They really put our backs up, strolling around Murrayfield as if they were the master race. We just wanted the game to start so that we could get stuck-in amongst them. I suppose it's unfortunate that everybody wants to beat the English — no I'm just saying that, it's not unfortunate at all — but they really don't do themselves any favours. They seem to invite the antagonism of the other rugby nations just by their superior attitude. It had been easy, then, to carry out our pre-match plan of building them up through our comments on the media. The English swallowed it hook, line and sinker.

It had already been decided that we would walk out to meet the enemy. It had even been suggested that we would be played on to the pitch by a piper but that was vetoed by the higher-ups. The walk itself, even without a piper, was just incredible. It had been the captain's idea and we all agreed. It was to be like a march, with the Scots going out to do battle with the Auld Enemy. Quite simply, I've never experienced anything like it. When we emerged from the tunnel the crowd started cheering and then, when they saw that we weren't galloping out as we normally did, they stopped cheering for just a second or two. Then, when they realised what we were doing, the cheering got louder, and louder and louder. It made the hairs stand up on the back of your neck. That set the tone for the afternoon and the crowd were like an extra man to us from then on.

David had already said his piece in the dressing-room before we went out. Again, like Geech, it was understated and hit the mark exactly. We were all clued in and every single one of us knew exactly what we had to do. Everybody has his own dressing-room ritual. I just like to sit quietly and gather myself. Damian Cronin is one of the game's big shouters. He stalks around the dressing-room bawling at the top of his voice. Scott Hastings isn't beyond the odd yell either. Soley, Fin, JJ and Gavin went round quietly and without fuss just speaking to everybody and making sure that they were thinking positively and focusing 100 per cent.

Then it was time to go. It was the most difficult thing imaginable to walk the thirty or forty yards from the dressing-room to the pitch. You have so much pent-up energy and emotion that you just want to pin back your ears and sprint out. But we managed it, to the kind of ear-splitting welcome that I've never experienced before or since.

The English players had already been out for a couple of minutes and we made them wait on purpose. Then we lined up for the anthems and, again, I've never heard anything like it before and probably never will again. Both verses of *Flower of Scotland* were sung for the first time. It's the best I've ever heard it sung. Usually, when you're standing in the middle of the pitch you hear on 'echo' as sections of the crowd get out of synch. But on Grand Slam Saturday everybody was with everybody else. It summed up the day and it was just brilliant. Whenever I watch that on video it brings tears to my eyes and I think it will continue to do that until the day that I die.

The first ten minutes of the game were a dream for us. We wanted quick penalties, quick lineouts, quick everything. That was the plan and it worked a treat. We were buzzing and the crowd was going crazy. The tone was set with a tap penalty that Fin drove on. He was stopped by, I think, Micky Skinner, but the boys got in behind Calder and drove the English ten metres up the park. Now the Englishmen knew that it wasn't going to be the pushover they thought it was going to be!

As I've said, we knew a lot of the English players from the previous year's Lions tour. It had been a good tour but, speaking personally, I found the English contingent very 'cliquey'. The Scots, Welsh and Irish had got along fine but the English tended to prefer their own company and would often disappear to play cards amongst themselves when the rest of us were getting on with the business of touring. So far as I was concerned, then, on Grand Slam Saturday I never thought that I was playing against mates — as I would have done if it had been Wales, and the likes of Robert Jones, that we had been playing — no, this was the Auld Enemy and I was keen to get in among them.

For the first half hour England were on the back foot. Scotland led 9–4 at half-time thanks to three penalty goals from Chic but we got a glimpse of what the English could do when Jerry Guscott strode away for a try. Guscott's touchdown gave the English their 'cockiness' back and they began to run stupid penalties, thinking, again, that the game was theirs for the taking. But it wasn't. They got us stuck on our line with a series of scrummages late in the first half. The English claim to this day that they should have had a penalty try because David Sole was repeatedly collapsing the scrum. I don't think that he was. He may have done once — when, very unsportingly, the English forwards rushed to take the scrum when we were a man down with Derek White off hurt and Derek Turnbull still to come on — but other than that I don't think the scrums were being brought down deliberately. In any case, the arrogance of the Englishmen proved to be their undoing. They were convinced that they were going to get a pushover try and so they were scrummaging penalties instead of going for goal. Brian Moore had obviously taken charge and the skipper Will Carling was just a spectator. Psychologically that was a huge turning-point in the game. England thought that they had the most powerful scrum in the Five Nations tournament but they came away from five or six minutes' pressure on our line with nothing to show for it.

I was quite relaxed at the interval. Geech had told me before the kick-off that I was to play my normal game. I was to harass the England scrum-half Richard Hill and their number 8 Mike Teague. I think I did that OK and at half-time I was happy enough.

In the second half our try came from a planned move which was codenamed Fiji. I had tried it already in the first half but it hadn't worked. In fact I got a bollocking from Gav because I hadn't drawn Rob Andrew on to me before releasing the ball. Basically, Fiji was a number 8 scrummage pick-up and I was then to draw the stand-off before passing to Gavin who would come into the line at speed, hopefully leaving our winger free and unmarked.

At the back of my mind was the telling-off that Gavin had given me in the first half and so as a result I made a wee half break and delayed the pass a bit. That drew Andrew and Teague on to me and so that was two English defenders taken out of the equation. I lobbed the ball out to Gavin — it wasn't much of a pass and he did well to hold on to it — and he put in a mighty chip for Tony Stanger to run on to and the rest is history.

The chip ahead wasn't originally part of the move but Geech always taught us that a planned move was just there to open the gap. After that you just have to play what was in front of you. Gav had good vision and improvised the kick ahead for Tony. If Stanger hadn't got the touchdown then Finlay was right there as well and so either way a try was very definitely on the cards.

It was an uphill struggle for England from then. They battled well but we defended better and they just had a penalty goal to show for their second-half efforts. The final ten minutes were unbelievable. England threw everything at us but we just weren't going to be beaten and we defended like our lives depended on it. People speak still of the tackle that Scott

Hastings put in on Guscott, but even if Scotty hadn't got him then, I believe, that Guscott would never have scored. The defence was three deep. After Scott came Gavin and me. There was no way that he was getting to the line.

We could still have been playing yet and I don't think that England would have scored. That Scottish team was unbeatable on the day. When the final whistle went, the feeling wasn't elation it was more relief. When we had all made it back to the dressing-room, through crowds of Scottish fans who were going wild with delight, it was, to be honest, quiet. We were all drained. I know I was. I was absolutely knackered, both physically and mentally. The medics were going around handing out the drinks but even at that stage we weren't saying much to each other. That was the biggest game that I've ever played in and, until the elation of victory had really sunk in, I have never felt so drained of energy. I was so tired that I could hardly lift an arm or a leg. They speak about 'dying for your country', well, I reckon that there were 16 guys who almost did that on Grand Slam Saturday. We had no more to give.

We had five minutes to ourselves just to gather our thoughts and to try to regain some of the energy we'd spent and then the coaches came in. It was Jim Telfer's fiftieth birthday and we all sang *Happy Birthday* and, OK the light was bad, but I could swear that I saw Jim smile!

After a quarter of an hour we got our second wind and the party began in earnest. Of course I knew that we had won the Grand Slam but it's only some time later, when you begin to put it in some historical perspective, that you can begin to appreciate what that really means to Scottish rugby. It was only the third time in the history of the Scottish game that it had happened and we were so proud to be part of it. We did it against England at Murrayfield and you really couldn't improve on that.

After we had dressed and were leaving the ground to go back into the centre of Edinburgh there was still a huge crowd waiting to cheer us on to the bus. And when we got to the Highland Carlton Hotel, where the official banquet was to be held, the team was given a standing ovation by all those who were waiting in the foyer and up on the balcony. The whole nation was stricken with Grand Slam fever. Geech had been right. Victory had meant everything, not just to the Scottish rugby community but to the Scottish nation as a whole. That day and team meant more to me than I could ever put into words. It's always a privilege and an honour to play for your country but to play in a Grand Slam side is something special and Saturday, 17 March 1990, is a day that will burn bright in my memory until the day that I die.

CHAPTER 6

LONG CLOUDS AND LONG STUDS

New Zealand 1990

NEW ZEALAND is still the cradle of world rugby. All Black sides come and All Black sides go. By their own standards some might not quite come up to the benchmarks set by their truly great XVs but of one thing there is no doubt. There is no such thing as a bad New Zealand team.

The strength of New Zealand rugby lies in their highly competitive provincial structure and, the cynics might say, in the manner in which the NZ game gets a regular transfusion of fresh talent from the South Seas and from the Polynesians who are attracted to the lifestyle in the land of the long white cloud.

Nevertheless, for true lovers of the game, New Zealand comes top of the list for touring. Off the pitch the people are warm and sincere. On the field — and no matter whether they are wearing that famous black shirt or representing their provinces — they play with a ruthless intensity that fairly takes the breath away.

There is no such thing as an easy game in New Zealand. I had been in Australia with the Lions in 1989 and would have to admit that some of the midweek opposition didn't really come up to scratch. That wasn't the case in New Zealand. Every game, midweek or not, had to be treated as a Test match.

Scotland travelled to New Zealand in the summer of 1990 with the Grand Slam tucked under our belts. We were the European champions. New Zealand, with their victory in the 1987 World Cup, were champions of the world. The tour had all the makings of the Ultimate Challenge in rugby, and so it proved.

That Scotland side was the best that I had been involved with. By the time the tour came around we had continued to improve on our performances in the Grand Slam season and we really were at the peak of our powers.

The tour opened with an easy 45–0 win over Poverty Bay-East Coast. But if we had entertained any thoughts about that match being a taster for what was to come then we were to be rapidly disabused of the notion. That was the only easy game on tour. After that they just got harder, and harder still.

I made my first appearance against Wellington. It was a tough old game against a hardened Provincial side and we did well to salvage a 16–16 draw. That was the game when John Jeffrey retired with what is known in these parts as a 'sair shooder' but, truth to tell, there was nothing wrong with his shoulder at all. He was hurt right enough but the shoulder didn't come into it.

JJ was walloped from behind by the Wellington lock Chris Tregaskis. It was a real coward's punch, a cheap shot from the rear at a lineout. We didn't really see what had happened but the aftermath was that John hit the deck like a felled tree. The coaches sitting on the sidelines had seen it all and the former Hawick, Scotland and British Lions flanker Derrick Grant told us later that Tregaskis should never have been allowed to finish the game in one piece.

JJ was completely out of it. He was away with the fairies. He didn't know whether he was in Wellington or Wichita. David Sole went over to him and John asked what was going on. Soley told him that he was playing rugby but he had hurt his shoulder and that he had better go off for treatment. I can laugh now but at the time JJ was badly concussed. He was taken straight back to the hotel by the doc and didn't play again for a fortnight.

Not that I really needed it but that incident underlined for me the entirely physical nature of rugby in New Zealand. I revelled in it but the Kiwi game is not one for the faint-hearted. At times it can be quite brutal. Certainly, Kiwis get away with murder from their refs when it comes to rucking. Their attitude is that if you are on the wrong side in a ruck, even if you are not impeding the ball and even if you are trying to get out of the way, then you are going to get a real shoeing and the refs don't seem to mind at all.

We weren't there very long before we decided that what was sauce for the goose was sauce for the gander as well. We were technically proficient at the rucking game — Jim Telfer and Derrick Grant had, after all, based the Scottish version on the New Zealand model — but we had to learn to be as ruthless in its execution as were the New Zealanders themselves.

We found that against touring sides anything went. If you go to New Zealand then every side that you come up against is playing for the honour of New Zealand. Of course we were proud to be playing for our country as well but rugby in NZ means almost everything to Kiwis. After all, nice country that it is, NZ doesn't really have much else going for it in a global sense. We discovered that, with home-based refs, the Provincial sides that we played got away with, almost but not quite, murder.

Some of the stuff that was going on was unbelievable. After the Wellington game the entire squad was pulled into a room at the team hotel and we were basically given a right bollocking by Ian McGeechan and Grant. We were losing players right, left and centre. Geech said that enough was enough and that if that was how they wanted to play against us then they would soon be in receipt of a double dose of their own medicine.

In particular Geech wanted us to get our rucking up to speed. As I've said, the New Zealanders were 'champing' into rucks with boots and studs flying. We were rucking hard, too, but we tended to be a bit more careful about where we placed our feet. Our forwards were told that from Wellington on we were taking no prisoners.

It had become apparent, too, that the New Zealand forwards were wearing illegal studs on their boots. That was the first time that I had seen them. They are made for Rugby League and they are longer and more pointed than their Rugby Union equivalents. They're OK in Rugby League because, of course, there isn't any rucking in the professional code. But in Union they were lethal. Normally if you're raked in a ruck then you get nasty scrapes on your torso or wherever but, most times, the skin isn't broken.

During our first couple of games in New Zealand we couldn't understand why our guys who had been rucked had actually been cut. It was like they had been slashed with a knife. I was rucked a few times and my body looked like a London Underground map. These illegal studs are worn for one reason only and that is to hurt the opposition. Referees know about them, of course, but sides that use them find it easy to hoodwink the ref when he comes to the dressing-room to check studs by showing him one pair of boots with legal studs and then wearing another pair for the game. Nevertheless, in New Zealand in 1990 we reckoned that, to survive, we had to fight fire with fire and a supply of Rugby League studs was made available to our forwards. Not everybody wore them but those that did gave as good as they got from then on in.

My next outing was againt Canterbury and I can say without fear of contradiction that this was the hardest, most bloody, most physical game of rugby that I have ever played in. We won 21–12 but the sheer physicality of the game took the breath away.

We knew that the Canterbury match was going to be a tough one and that it would give us a real indication as to how good we really were. Lancaster Park is an intimidating arena and Canterbury like nothing better than giving touring sides the once-over. They had a good side. Steve and Graeme Bachop, Andy Earl, Warwick Taylor, Dallas Seymour and Arthur Anderson were included in their line-up and so we knew that we faced a tough test of our mettle.

We were well prepared for what was to come but even so the brutality was of an order that many of us hadn't seen before. The Canterbury rucking was positively brutal. There was no finesse to it. Basically they were just kicking the shit out of you. Early on I tackled one of the Canterbury players and got caught on the wrong side of a ruck. I was trapped and couldn't get out of the way and the whole Canterbury pack just trampled all over me.

I got a real kicking from Seymour and Anderson. My old guardian Fin Calder came to my rescue as he had done on many occasions before and, in fact, dished out some retribution of his own when he shoulder-charged Arthur Anderson and bust the All Black's ribs. It was perfectly legal and above board. Anderson was lurking with intent on the wrong side of a ruck and Fin caught him with his shoulder in the rib cage. Raw-boned is the perfect description for Calder and if you are shoulder-charged by him then you are going to know all about it. Certainly Anderson knew all about it that day at Lancaster Park. He left the field in agony and we never saw him again in the tour.

Having said all of that I would have to admit that I enjoyed the game tremendously. Maybe I would have felt differently if we hadn't come out on the winning side but we had taken them on up front and we had won. It was very satisfying.

I have concentrated thus far on the negative side of the game in New Zealand but I wouldn't like to give the impression that it was a trip which I didn't enjoy. On the contrary, I loved it. I revelled in the physicality of their game and admired the way that New Zealand players would, almost, have died for their Province or their country. In 1990 they were the World Champions and they fully deserved that accolade for their dedication to the concept of total rugby. That's not the first thing on your mind, though, when you're lying at the bottom of a ruck and an 18-stone All Black is performing a tap dance on your head!

Off the field, the New Zealanders were absolutely superb. It is the best country that I have ever toured. They really like the Scots in New Zealand and we really appreciated the hospitality that they showed us. On the park they might have wanted to rip off your head but once the game was over the Kiwis showed themselves to be some of the most hospitable folk on earth. In fact I found New Zealand to be very similar in many respects to Scotland and my own Border country. On the field you knock lumps out of each other but once the final whistle has gone then you can have a crack and a laugh together in the bar.

As I've said, the previous year I had been in Australia with the British Lions and, comparing one country with the other, there was no contest. New Zealand left Australia at the starting gate when it came to rugby and in the way that we were treated as players and individuals. I also found the spectators to be some of the most knowledgeable that I have ever met and I would have no hesitation in saying to any youngster who wants to further his rugby education that New Zealand is the place to do so.

At the end of the tour I was asked by Taranaki if I wanted to stay on and play for them. They offered to fly the family out from Scotland and provide accommodation and all the rest. I have to admit that the offer was tempting but, come the end of a gruelling rugby campaign, all that most of the guys want to do is to get on that plane for home.

The next game was midweek against Southland. I was on the bench as Brewster's Beezers — so called in honour of the midweek skipper Alex Brewster — won 45–12. Our confidence was on a high and we went into the first Test just four days later confident that we could take the All Blacks to the wire.

But we never really got it together. We made far too many unforced errors and made things easy for the Kiwis. It was a day, too, that Iwan Tukalo would rather forget. The All Blacks scored two tries on his wing and he was dropped for Alex Moore in the second Test a week later. Iwan knew that he hadn't played well and he showed a great deal of character to come back from his disappointment and to win back his place in the Scottish side.

That kicking machine Grant Fox put the All Blacks into an early lead with a penalty goal. Then we struck back with a try by Sean Lineen. It was a big moment for Sean — a Scot by choice and a Kiwi by birth — to score against his other 'ain folk'. Chris

Gray, who played some of the best rugby of his life on that tour, also had a try and it really did look for a while as if we were going to beat the All Blacks for the first time in Scottish rugby history.

Thereafter, though, our game went to pieces and we made far too many unforced errors. The All Blacks ran out winners 31–16 and although the scoreline flattered them we knew that we hadn't done enough to deserve the win. I was desperately disappointed because, like the rest of the team, we really did think that we were good enough to have beaten the New Zealanders.

Brewster's Beezers had an outing against Manawatu before the second Test in Auckland and although they didn't play as well as they had done against Southland they still did enough to win 19–4 and keep alive our record of not having lost to a provincial side.

By then, though, all thoughts were on the second Test match. We reckoned that we had given the All Blacks too much respect in Dunedin. There is no doubt that the All Blacks do have a mystique about them but, at the end of the day, they just have two arms and two legs like the rest of us and they are there to be knocked off their perch just like any other side.

We had taken a close look at the video recording of the first Test and it confirmed what we already knew about the lineout. We had given Ian Jones an easy ride for his first cap and New Zealand had dominated on the touchlines. Damian Cronin was the experienced man and he should have taken the Kammo Kid to the cleaners. In the second Test we 'double-jumped' Jones, putting two men on to him, and he didn't enjoy nearly the same free run that he had got first time around.

Also we knew that we had to eliminate the unforced errors. We were still confident that we could square the series and when we went 15 points up it looked like that first win against the All Blacks was about to become a reality. The opening half hour of that game saw Scotland play the best rugby that I have ever been involved with. It was right up there with our Grand Slam performance against England. We gave away a try just before half-time when the All Blacks got up a head of steam with a rolling maul which started on our 22 and ended with them scoring at the posts. That was the turning-point of the Test match. We lost 21–18 but we had outscored them two tries to one and there were some bitterly disappointed Scots when the final whistle went.

On two occasions the All Blacks got lucky. I was involved in the first incident when I had to leave the field for treatment to a damaged left knee. I had been 'champed' earlier on and the knee was bloody sore but then the All Black prop Richard Loe stood on the same knee in the exact same spot. It was absolute agony. I didn't want to leave the field and was in tears by the time I reached the dressing-room. There were only nine minutes to go and I didn't want to leave the boys when we were playing so well.

Anyway, while I was being led away there was a scrum near the corner flag and Fin got caught offside. Grant Fox, as always, was right on target with the penalty kick and that was an easy three points in the bag for them. The knee was taped up but it was too sore to continue and Greig Oliver came on as sub for me. Then Gavin Hastings was penalised for not releasing the ball after a garryowen by Fox. He was tackled by Mike Brewer from what seemed at first to have been a blatantly offside position. However, watching the video since, I reckon that maybe Brewer was observing the 10-metre rule but he was played back onside by Gav taking a few steps out of the cordon area. Whatever, the end result was another dose of easy points for the New Zealanders.

Afterwards the boys were really emotional. There were quite a few tears shed. You could have heard a pin drop in the dressing-room. The manager Duncie Paterson went around trying to cheer us up but we all knew that the win had been there for the taking and we had let it slip from our grasp. Scotland have never beaten the All Blacks in 90 years of trying. To have lowered their colours on their own patch would have been some mean achievement. We came within three points of doing it. It was close, but still no cigar!

CHAPTER 7

WORLD IN UNION

Rugby World Cup 1991

THE WORLD CUP has changed the face of rugby forever. Before the advent of the competition in 1987, the biggest thing that most players had to look forward to was a British Lions' tour. There is still, to my way of thinking, a place in the ever expanding world of rugby for the Lions which command a special place in the hearts and minds of rugby folk all over the globe. But as a sporting spectacular which grabs the attention of even the non-rugby fraternity, there is no doubt that the World Cup now occupies centre-stage.

In comparison to the 1991 tournament in which I took part — and even more so compared to the 1995 version with which I dearly wish I had been involved — the inaugural event in 1987, staged in New Zealand and Australia and won by the All Blacks, now looks like a village fête. It was a real toe-in-the-water job. The TV contract was signed only at the last minute and, even in countries where rugby was a recognised sport, the viewing figures didn't exactly set the heather on fire.

By the time the 1991 tournament came around the whole shooting match was conducted on a much more professional basis. The tournament, rather messily spread out over Scotland, England, Ireland, Wales and France — just as it will be again in

1999 — was without doubt the biggest sporting event of the year and ranking only behind the Olympic Games and the soccer World Cup in size.

Once again the world's top 16 nations did battle for the William Webb Ellis Cup and the 32 games were watched by over one million spectators, while a cumulative audience of nearly two billion watched on television in 70 countries. It's only when you consider figures like these that you realise just how the game of rugby has arrived on the world stage and you begin to appreciate the huge revenues that the game now attracts.

Scotland had been handed a dream draw. We were in a pool alongside Ireland, Zimbabwe and Japan and — even more encouragingly — we were scheduled to play all of our pool matches at Murrayfield. The fact that we were to perform on our own patch meant that we would start each game with points on the board. In those days Fortress Murrayfield really meant something. We just didn't lose home games and the support of the Murrayfield crowd provided us with the equivalent of an extra man.

Our preparation for the World Cup, which was played throughout October and early November, began months beforehand when we were provided with fitness schedules to work on throughout the summer. Scotland were touring America and Canada in the early summer but most of the senior players opted to stay at home and work on their fitness in readiness for the major RWC test which most of us considered more important than the North American tour.

The coaching team of Ian McGeechan, Derrick Grant, Jim Telfer and Dougie Morgan had arranged a number of warm-up games but, truth to tell, the warm-up got just a bit too hot for comfort. Just a month or so before we were due to play Japan in the opening game of the World Cup we jetted off to Bucharest to take on Romania in what should have been a testing, but very definitely winnable, encounter. We lost. The entire weekend was a nightmare. Romania was still in the process of recovering from the revolution and amenities were, to put it kindly, basic. The

Scottish Rugby Union, aware of the fact that everything was in short supply in Bucharest, made sure that we took our own food with us. Even so it had to be cooked locally in our hotel and lots of guys came down with Bucharest belly. Taking the rough with the smooth is very much part of touring but Romania in 1991 was very much a case of taking the rough with the rough.

We weren't in the best of shape when we ran out on to the turf at the 23 August Stadium in downtown Bucharest and the Romanians, who were suitably fired up for the occasion, proceeded to put a dent in our World Cup plans by winning 18–12. It was just one of those games where nothing went right. The harder we tried the worse it became and, to tell the truth, the Romanians were better than their six-point winning margin suggested.

But our problems didn't end there. The flight home was another nightmare. We were flying courtesy of the Romanian state airline and very soon it began to resemble the airline from hell. Soon after take-off in Bucharest we were forced to make an emergency landing at a military airfield after the plane developed a fault.

We were herded into a large room where we were to remain for a couple of hours and more. Then, when we were eventually allowed back on to the aeroplane, all of the big forwards were told to go and sit at the rear. At first we thought it was a wind-up but they were deadly serious. They said there was a fault with the front end and, please, would all of the big men move to the back of the aircraft. So Damian Cronin and John Jeffrey and all the big men trooped off to the rear leaving us little guys at the front. I was never so glad to see the green, green grass of home and be able to put Bucharest behind me.

A week later Scotland played the Barbarians at Murrayfield. The Baa-Baas were coming to the end of their centenary season and they had spread the net far and wide to field a really strong side. The South African André Joubert, who was to be such an influential player in the Springboks' RWC 1995 triumph, was at full-back, the half-back pairing was Pierre Berbizier and Stuart

Barnes and, in the pack, there was a formidable front-row trio of Guy Kebble, Tom Lawton and Enrique Rodrigues plus the likes of Eric Rush and Wahl Bartmann in the back row. I sat on the bench as Greig Oliver took over the duties at scrum-half and it was clear to me from very early on that these Barbarians hadn't come to Murrayfield to play their traditional champagne rugby. This was real, hard Test rugby and the boys did extremely well to hold the Barbarians to a 16–16 draw.

For the next couple of games we changed guise to appear as an SRU President's XV. We beat the Anglo-Scots 32–4 but the name change did little to aid our somewhat mixed fortunes.

Immediately prior to coming together as a permanent squad and bussing off to St Andrews, where we would base ourselves for much of the RWC tournament, we played Edinburgh Borderers at Murrayfield. The Borderers, led by a very fired-up Jeremy Richardson who had come back uncapped from the 1987 World Cup campaign and who had failed to make the squad for the 1991 version, beat us 13–9 and our preparations had ended, just as they had begun, in defeat.

However, we weren't as disheartened as might have been thought. These warm-up type games are very difficult to take part in. Most players, with an eye on the big prize coming up, are very wary of getting injured. Of course everybody knows that it's at times like those — when you are desperate to steer clear of injury – that you will get hurt. But that doesn't make it any easier. When we played Edinburgh Borderers most of us were — in our minds at least — already on the bus to St Andrews. But that's not to diminish the effort of Richardson and his side who could claim, with some justification, that they were the unofficial fourth-placed team in the world.

The month-long duration of the World Cup was a funny time for us. To all intents and purposes we were on tour but it was like no tour we had ever been on before. We were on tour in our own country. It was strange to know that your home and your family were just an hour away unlike normally where you are thousands of miles from home. The management kept us fresh by providing us with two bases. We used the superb Old Course Hotel, overlooking the seventeenth fairway at St Andrews, as our 'out of town' base and then we would use the Dalmahoy Hotel and Country Club just outside Edinburgh around match days.

The system worked well as it allowed us a change of scenery. There's nothing worse than being couped up in the same place for weeks on end, even if you are wallowing in five-star luxury.

The core of the squad we took into the World Cup campaign was still that which had taken the Grand Slam the year before. Finlay Calder, who had said that he would call it a day after the summer tour to New Zealand in 1990, had been coaxed out of retirement and, throughout the World Cup, he played as well as he had ever done. John Jeffrey was calling it a day after the World Cup and Derek White, the third member of Scotland's best ever back-row unit, would play just one more season so this was very much the swansong of the Calder, White, Jeffrey trio.

One of the main attractions of the World Cup for me is the fact that it is a knock-out competition. If you don't produce the goods then you are out. There are no second chances. Our schedule was going to be tough enough. We had Japan on the opening Saturday, followed by Zimbabwe on the Wednesday and, then, Ireland the following Saturday.

Against Japan we weren't taking anything for granted. We knew that they had been in a training camp for over a month prior to the World Cup and that, whenever they gained possession, they would run the ball at us as if there was no tomorrow. Their major problem is their size. They are just too small to compete at world level but they compensate with hearts as big as barrage balloons. The Japanese threw everything at us bar the kitchen sink and we led by only 17–9 at the interval. Gradually, though, we began to take command and ran out winners by 47–9. We certainly knew we had been in a game. Craig Chalmers received a blow to the throat which left him groggy and he was replaced by Douglas Wyllie with ten minutes to go. Also, David Sole gashed an ear when he collided with John

Jeffrey, allowing David Milne — the third of the Bear brothers — to come on for his first cap and to complete the family treble, joining Iain and Kenny among the ranks of Scottish international forwards. But the courage of the Japanese was best summed up by an amazing tackle that their centre, Katsuki, put in on Scott Hastings. Scott was powering down the touchline in front of the old West Stand and he must have reckoned that he was home and dry.

Then, out of nowhere, Katsuki appeared like a rocket to shoulder-charge Scotty into touch. The sound of the collision must have registered like an earthquake on the Richter scale and both players fell to the ground like sacks of potatoes. The sight of the wee Japanese boy thundering across the field and running full pelt into Scott will always be one of the memories that I take away from my rugby career and, for me, it underlined what the game should be about. Never mind the fact that the Japanese were well beaten. They never gave up, their heads never went down and, despite the fact that they are almost always thrashed when they come up against the big Westerners, they always come back for more.

We were relieved to have got the first game out of the way and we celebrated long into the night. At the dinner afterwards we initiated the Japanese into the 'drinking game' custom. Goodness only knows what the Japanese made of 'Buzz' and 'Zip-Boyng'. Craig was one of the leading instigators but, as the night wore on, he paid the customary price for over-indulging in red wine and port. As I've said elsewhere, it is the camaraderie of the game that most attracts me to Rugby Union. Despite the fact that I don't speak Japanese and the Japanese would be hard-pressed to understand my 'Jethart' English, we had a great night, both teams enjoying the 'crack' and the post-match fun which makes rugby special.

Zimbabwe were next. Greig Oliver played in this one and I sat on the bench. We eventually won 51–12 after a tentative start, Iwan Tukalo scoring a hat-trick before going off hurt and being replaced by Craig just a minute before the end. With his first touch of the ball Chic set off on a 40-metre run. He hadn't really had time to warm up properly before being called on as a replacement and those of us on the bench were all shouting for him to kick the ball out of play in case he pulled a hamstring. That was the last thing we needed. However, all was well that ended well and, with two wins, we had made sure of qualifying for the quarter-finals.

Nevertheless, we still had a lot to play for. If we wanted to continue our run at Murrayfield then we had to beat our next opponents, Ireland. If we lost then we would be going to Lansdowne Road. Therefore the incentive to continue our winning run against Ireland was significant indeed.

The Irish are never easy opponents. They only know of one way to play and that is at 100 miles an hour. In the 1991 Five Nations Championship we had beaten them 28–25 at Murrayfield after a massive struggle and so we knew that we would be pretty evenly matched.

The Irishmen gave us a real hard time of it but we eventually got their measure and ran out winners 24–15. However, we didn't survive entirely unscathed. Due to a mistake by me Chic got 'cairted' when he was tackled heavily and had to leave the field with a 'dead leg'. It was a momentary lapse in concentration on my part which got Chalmers into trouble. I was under no pressure whatsoever at a scrum and I sent out a dud pass to Chic. The Irish flanker Gordon Hamilton arrived at about the same time as the ball and he caught Chic with a 'right sair yin'. He had to hobble off and his Melrose clubmate Graham Shiel came on to win his first cap. After just ten minutes or so, he had scored a try. It was a dream début for young Shiellie who has really come on in leaps and bounds in recent years and, by the time of the 1995 World Cup was, virtually, the pick of the Scotland backs.

In addition to Craig, Sean Lineen was also 'crocked' against the Irish. He had suffered a boot to the knee and the blow was so severe that the knee-cap was dislodged. There was now some doubt as to whether Craig, and in particular Sean, would be fit in time for our quarter-final tie against Western Samoa. Here, space-age technology came to their aid. The SRU rustled up a hyperbaric-oxygen chamber from somewhere and the pair of them were condemned to spend long periods inside so as to aid recovery. Don't ask me how it works but it did the trick for Chic who was back on duty for Western Samoa although Sean would have to wait until our semi-final showdown against the Auld Enemy before he was passed fit enough for action.

Despite the injuries the match was fairly, yet fiercely, contested. However, immediately it was over a huge controversy blew up over a Finlay Calder tackle on the Irish full-back Jim Staples. From a scrum just inside the Irish half, I had sent up a high ball which fell perfectly. Tony Stanger arrived just as Staples was fielding the ball. Tony held him and just seconds later Fin arrived going at full lick. Fin's left shoulder caught Staples on the head and the Irishman hit the deck. Afterwards, there was a great hue and cry about dangerous play by Calder. There were allegations in the press that Fin had forearm-smashed Staples to the ground. Frankly, that's nonsense. I've watched the incident on video since then and I still reckon that it was a perfectly fair challenge. It was a 'top and tail' tackle with Calder at the top and Stanger at the tail. It does appear as if Fin is bringing around his left arm in a punching motion but the camera angle is deceptive. The shoulder charge was one of the main weapons in Calder's armoury. The Kiwi Arthur Anderson had discovered that to his cost in New Zeland the year before and, nearer to home, Fin's bony shoulder had almost cost the skipper David Sole his place in our RWC campaign when, in a training accident just days beforehand, he had caught David in the kidneys to such a severe extent that it caused bruising and internal bleeding. Fin's shoulder charge, then, as Soley, Anderson and, now Staples, had discovered was to be avoided at all costs.

Finlay got a lot of stick after that incident and was on the receiving end of a lot of hate-mail. I still don't reckon that the tackle was illegal but, as subsequent events were to prove, I reckon that Staples was undoubtedly concussed and should have left the field.

Poor Staples was still groggy when we won a lineout just outside the Irish 22. I sent up another high ball not, I think, with the absolute intention of testing Staples again but mainly because the forwards had given me rubbish ball and there wasn't a lot more to do with it than to send it into the air over their heads. If, as a scrum-half, you always aim to put the ball in front of the forwards then you'll never go far wrong. Nevertheless, I saw right away when Staples came for the ball that he still wasn't right. He completely misjudged his attempted catch and the ball bounced off his right shoulder. Graham Shiel scooped up the loose ball and was over for the try, his first in international rugby. Gavin's conversion made it 15–15 and, gradually, we were getting ourselves into the driving seat.

After watching Staples make a hash of that high ball I reckoned that he was fair-game from then on in and in fact the try which I scored came from targeting him. Graham Shiel, this time, put Staples under the high ball and he was engulfed by Scottish tacklers. Fin pounced on the loose ball, Chris Gray popped it up to me, I popped it to Tony before looping him and going over for a try at the post. It was undoubtedly ruthless of us to have made so much capital out of Staples's misfortune but this was serious stuff not a Sunday afternoon 'bounce' game in the park. This was international rugby and if Staples wasn't well, as he obviously wasn't, then he should have gone off. Nevertheless, I was amazed at the fuss that blew up in the papers afterwards. Immediately after the game not one of the Irish players mentioned either the Calder tackle or the fact that we had taken advantage of the situation which Staples found himself in. I'm sure that if the boot had been on the other foot then they would have responded in exactly the same manner. It was only the media that made a big thing of it and only when we read the Sunday papers did we realise that there had been any kind of controversy at all.

However, we had maintained our 100 per cent record and we were scheduled to play the Western Samoans in the Murrayfield quarter-final. The Samoans had been the sensation of the tournament. They had arrived as rank outsiders and had qualified for their pool in Wales along with Australia at the expense of Argentina, and unbelievably, the home side. Wales were really in the toils. Their defeat meant that they had to go through the indignity of qualification for the 1995 tournament.

The big feature of the Western Samoan play had been their tackling. It was of the 'no prisoners' variety and, schooled as most of them were in the New Zealand provincial set-up they were a very talented side indeed. In fact, when you ignored the fact that they came from string of small islands in the South Pacific with a population of not more than 170,000, but concentrated on the fact that, almost to a man, they played their rugby in New Zealand, then it became easier to understand just why they made such an impact in 1995. They were, to all intents and purposes, the New Zealand 'B' team and not at all the underdogs that they appeared at first sight.

They came to Murrayfield with the intention of taking us on physically. However, we were more than capable of playing them at their own game and, in fact, that's just what we did. In training beforehand it was decided that we would play it hard and tight and that we would bring Gavin Hastings in at every opportunity on short, sharp balls from scrums, rucks and mauls. We wanted to meet fire with fire and bringing Gavin in, basically from the stand-off position, meant that he provided a physical presence in the rough and tumble of rucks and mauls on which our forwards could work.

Basically the strategy worked like a dream. The Western Samoans never knew what hit them. They were forced to swallow some of their own medicine and, in the first half particularly, our pack played some of the best rugby that I've ever seen. In addition, Scott Hastings showed that the Samoans weren't the only team who could tackle and by the end we had logged an entirely convincing 28–6 win. It was a superb game in which to have played and at the end the Murrayfield crowd showed that they had thoroughly enjoyed it as well with the ovation they gave to the Samoans as their skipper Peter Fatialofa led them on a farewell lap of honour.

That same afternoon, England won their torrid quarter-final clash againt France at Parc des Princes and the stage was set for a semi-final duel at Murrayfield against the Auld Enemy. So far as the English were concerned there were some old scores to settle. The last time they had been at Murrayfield, on 17 March 1990, they had been forced to eat humble pie when they had fallen foul of their own arrogance and some inspired Scottish play. It had cost them 'their' Grand Slam and they were desperate for revenge.

This was one of the most physically demanding games that I've played in. The English decided to keep the ball tight and to build the game around their huge pack. It was dull and it was boring but, eventually, it was effective. They won 9–6 by virtue of two John Webb penalty goals and a Rob Andrew drop-goal to two penalties by Gavin. Leaving aside the recent history of games between Scotland and England there was a huge incentive for both of us to perform to the top of our abilities. A place in the World Cup final isn't something that comes along very often and we gave our all in an effort to make it ours.

We led 6–0 thanks to Gav's penalty goals and Webb, who was having a nightmare with the boot, eventually managed to put one over to make it 6–3 at half-time. Webb kicked another in the second half to level terms and then came the moment that Gav has described as the worst in his rugby life.

With 20 minutes to go we were awarded a penalty just to the right of the posts. In fact it was so slightly to the right that, to all intents and purposes, the kick was slap-bang in front of the uprights. It was just 20 metres out and it was a kick that you could bet your life that Gavin would slot home ninety-nine times out of a hundred. Sadly, this was the one time in a hundred that he missed. The ball just slid around the right upright. It was just six inches wide of the mark but it may as well have been six feet. I couldn't believe it.

The kick would have given us a 9–6 lead. It didn't by any stretch of the imagination mean that we would have been home and dry but it would have helped. However, Gavin shouldn't under any circumstances be blamed. His kicking had saved us so many times and had contributed so much to our progress in this tournament that one lapse didn't mean that he had to shoulder the blame for our defeat.

There is a tremendous amount of pressure on a goal-kicker. It's certainly not a task that I would like to undertake. And at international level, in front of thousands and before a TV audience of millions, there is no such thing as an easy kick. We played our guts out in an effort to bounce back but it all came to nothing when, with just five minutes remaining, Rob Andrew dropped the goal that took England to the final. It could so easily have been us but 'if onlys' count for nothing. England had ground out a victory that must have been murder for the spectators to endure but they, and not us, would be going to Twickenham to take on the Australians.

We had wanted to win so badly for the likes of John Jeffrey and Finlay who were playing their last games at Murrayfield but we just couldn't bring it off. What lay in store for us was the third-place play-off in Cardiff against New Zealand. I don't hold with the theory that the play-off game is a game too many. It's surely better to finish third than fourth. The way I looked at it, it wasn't every day that you got to play against the All Blacks and I was as 'up' for the game as any of the others that I've played in a Scotland jersey.

We had, of course, come close to beating the All Blacks the previous summer in New Zealand and before the game I certainly looked upon it as another 'extra' opportunity to create Scottish rugby history by taking an All Black scalp. But, once again, it was not to be.

It was a hard, physical game. They won 13–6 and we had to settle for the bronze medals. Once again Fin was in the wars, this time for a real beaut of a head-butt on the Kiwi skipper Sean Fitzpatrick. It looked worse than it was because Fin never really made contact but what the onlookers didn't see was the reason for it. I was lying at the bottom of a ruck and Fitzpatrick was tap-dancing on my head. Fin had been my 'minder' since the day I arrived in the Scotland side and he maintained the tradition right up to the day he retired.

Two other incidents come to mind. One was the superb bodycheck that Gavin put on All Black prop Richard Loe. Gav charged upfield, led with the shoulder and swept the New Zealand hard-man aside like he was a seven-stone weakling. The second memory is not quite so sweet. In fact it cost us the game. We were still well in with a chance of victory until almost the end when we were awarded a penalty inside our own 22. Craig decided to take a quick tap and he passed the ball on to me. The New Zealand flanker Michael Jones flattened me, the ball went loose and Walter Little ran in for the try. David Sole wasn't over-pleased that Chic had taken it upon himself to run the ball instead of booting it down into New Zealand territory but it was almost full-time and if we had run the length of the pitch to score the winning try then we would have been heroes. Some you win and some you lose. However, I reckon we had acquitted ourselves well. We hadn't disgraced ourselves but that horrible statistic of no Scottish side ever having beaten the All Blacks still stood to be challenged again another day. Hopefully, I'll be around to have another crack at it in 1996 in New Zealand.

So, all that remained was for us to attend the Twickenham final as all-expenses-paid spectators. And here we got ourselves into more trouble. Who were we supporting? Australia of course. We bought Wallaby scarves from stalls in the Twickenham car park and we wore them with pride as we took our seats in the stand.

The English players hated us for that. It rankles still with them. But who did they expect us to support? They didn't seriously think that we'd come down to Twickenham showing 'Northern Hemisphere solidarity' and backing them against the Australians after they had put us out. No way. I've got news for them. Even the New Zealanders, whose rivalry with Australia is just as fierce as ours is with England, were wearing Aussie favours.

England, for the first time in the tournament — some would say for the first time in living memory — tried to play expansive rugby and they lost. With clever use of the media, David Campese and the Australian management had conned the English into setting aside their powerhouse game plan which was based around the pack. Australia won 12–6 and the William Webb Ellis Cup was Sydney bound. We went back home to Scotland, happy enough with our fourth place but mindful, too, that we had come so close to getting to the final and that, once there, the sky would have been the limit.

CHAPTER 8

THE GREAT DIVIDE

League Comes Calling

IF I had a fiver for every time that I've been asked the question 'Why didn't you sign up for Rugby League?' then maybe I wouldn't be rich but I'd certainly have a substantial wad of notes to slap on the bar at Riverside Park and more than enough to keep the boys well supplied for an 'interesting' Saturday night.

It was a topic which always came up whenever I did press interviews. I preferred to keep them guessing. But the fact of the matter is that Rugby League clubs were frequent callers and on one occasion I was just a signature on a contract short of making the colossal step from the 'amateur' ranks of Union into the professional world of Rugby League. The gulf between the two codes is still one of the great divides in sport. It doesn't matter that 'amateur' union is no longer the great amateur game it used to be. At that time once you had made the decision to enlist within the legitimately paid ranks it was almost as if you had signed on with a rival tribe.

The Scottish Borders have always been one of the happiest of hunting-grounds for Rugby League sides. At the beginning of the century, when Rugby Union was getting itself established in the Border towns, clubs were constantly losing their best players to professional raiders from south of the Border. On a lesser scale the trend continues to this day. Of course Scotland hasn't suffered anything like the same kind of ravaging which has gone on in Wales where, for generations, the Principality's best players have taken the road 'Up North'. Within the last decade Wales has lost virtually an entire national side to the predators of the professional code.

In Wales, just as in the Borders, Rugby Union is a game for the working man. It's easy to see, therefore, why players from both localities found the offer of being paid for something they love doing an attractive proposition.

Rugby League was born out of a row over 'broken time payments'. In Yorkshire, where the Union game was predominantly working class, the clubs were more than willing to recompense their players for taking time off work to play. In London and the Home Counties, where the game was played by the toffs and the professional classes, this was frowned upon as being contrary to the spirit of the game.

It was in 1895, following a meeting at the George Hotel in Huddersfield, that eleven of the north of England's principal clubs resigned from the Yorkshire Union to form the breakaway Northern Union. The separation had been bad-tempered and the 'class' factor had played a significant role in the debate. Professional rugby had arrived and the rivalries which have lasted a century and more were born.

Right from the start Union and League didn't get on. When you understand just how bitter the split had been then you can begin to appreciate why the two branches of the oval-ball game still don't get along particularly well today.

So far as the game itself is concerned I can take it or leave it. There's not nearly so much going on in a League match as there is in Rugby Union. But what they do, they do well. League players handle and tackle better than most Union players but that's only because League is such a limited game that they handle and tackle more than we do. Practice does make perfect. We often play League on training nights at Riverside Park. It keeps you sharp and there's no doubt that it does hone your handling and tackling skills and it does make you think more about your running angles.

Whenever a Union player moves across to League people speak about it as a 'defection', as if you're somehow letting the side down. I don't see it that way at all. When Alan Tait, the Kelso and Scotland centre, signed for Widnes in 1988, Borderers certainly didn't see it that way. They just thought, good luck to him, he's going to make some money for himself and for his family. Alan had been capped for Scotland during the World Cup in 1987 and played in the Five Nations tournament the following year. We played together for Scotland in the Australian bi-centennial sevens tournament and he told me then that he was going to Rugby League. His father had been a League player and I think that Alan was always destined for the legitimately paid ranks and so his move to Widnes didn't come as a surprise to me, or to many Borderers. His move generated a lot of interest in the Borders and even yet busloads of Borderers regularly make the trip south to watch him play.

Since then Alan has really made his mark. He has transferred to Leeds and has become a regular in the Great Britain side. People have often said to me — and Alan was among them — that with my style of play I was tailor-made for Rugby League. That may well be the case but the down side, so far as I was concerned, was that you would very much be in the position of being told what to do for almost every moment of the day. I've never been a great trainer. I have been lucky in that I'm blessed with a high degree of natural fitness and I never took kindly to the strict fitness regimes which the Scotland squad were subjected to. I was always fit enough to play international rugby but I looked upon training very much as a necessary chore. It wasn't something that I enjoyed. Some of my Scotland colleagues trained every single day in life. I never did. I trained with the club on Tuesdays and Thursdays and with the Scottish squad on Sundays. That was more than enough for me. As a full-time professional in League you would be expected to be slogging away almost seven days a week. The prospect didn't appeal to me. So that was the down side of Rugby League so far as I was concerned. Also, I was keen to remain in Jedburgh. I'm a hometown boy and was never happier than when I was amongst my 'ain folk' at Jed.

Nevertheless, on a fairly regular basis I would have Rugby League scouts on the telephone asking if I was interested in switching codes. Before he left Widnes for Leeds, Alan Tait called me asking if I would be interested in an official approach. At the time I had just broken through into the Scottish national side, I was just about to get married to Shona and had been picked for the British Lions tour to Australia. When I returned from that tour the telephone lines were hot again with League people inquiring if I would be interested in joining them.

And then Carlisle came on the scene. They approached brother Kevin first of all. Kevin is a very fine back-row player in his own right. At one stage in our careers he had more Scotland age-group caps than I did and, of course, he finally made the breakthrough into the senior Scotland squad when he went on tour with them to the South Seas in 1993. Unfortunately, his tour was disrupted by injury but he had obviously caught the eye of the Carlisle Rugby League club which was then on a major recruiting drive.

Kevin was interested in making the move and then Carlisle made a play for me as well and I was very definitely interested. They were a Division II side and weren't playing at the high standard of some of the other clubs which had beaten a path to my door but their situation just south of the Border meant that my main concern about switching codes would no longer be a factor.

Carlisle was just an hour and a half from Jed and they were offering the kind of money that made the deal attractive from a financial point of view as well. I was to be allowed to live in Jed and travel down for training and games therefore Kevin and I entered into negotiations in earnest.

The ball started rolling towards the end of 1991. Kevin was still unmarried and living with our parents in Berwick. The initial approach took place when a Carlisle director, Frank Lowe, phoned my dad. They inquired first of all about Kevin's availability. Initially he turned them down and we thought that was the end of the matter but Carlisle were nothing if not insistent and they upped the offer. From Kevin's point of view it then became an attractive proposition. He was just about to get married and was looking for a house of his own. It made sense to think of starting a whole new life by getting married and signing professional forms both at the same time.

In the course of the negotiations with Kevin my name came up and the two of us talked it over. We've always been close and the prospect of us playing for Carlisle together was one that we didn't want to walk away from without exploring all the possibilities.

We then embarked upon a series of secret meetings, some of which were held at Mosspaul Hotel, the old coaching inn on the Hawick-Carlisle road. As a venue for a clandestine meeting it was perfect. It was midway between Jed and Carlisle and, at that time of the year, set as it is deep in the Border hills, it was quiet and secluded.

It wasn't cloak-and-dagger stuff. Kevin and I and my dad just met the Carlisle representatives over a drink. We didn't go out of our way to publicise the fact that we were negotiating terms to switch codes. But neither did we slip in and out of the hotel in disguise and under cover of darkness. It soon became clear that Carlisle had been watching us for a while. And on one occasion, a floodlit game between Jed and Kelso, they actually phoned to say that they were coming to have another look at Kevin.

In January 1992, while all of this was going on, I suffered the first of my serious knee injuries, playing for Jed against Currie at Riverside Park. Carlisle weren't put off by the fact that things look pretty dodgy and merely insisted that when we resumed negotiations they would like me to undergo a strict medical carried out by their own doctor.

For the first two months of 1992 the negotiations went on between us and the Carlisle chairman Alan Tucker, Frank Lowe and coach Cameron Bell. Eventually, on 4 February, 1992, it got to the stage of draft contracts. In return for relinquishing my amateur status Carlisle were offering a five-year deal with a tax-free signing-on fee of £25,000.

Additionally, on an annual basis, from which tax and national insurance would be deducted, I was to receive £20,000 a season until 1996–97. On top of this I was to get £250 for each six first-team appearances I made with the club, plus a regulation player's weekly wage of £90 for a win and £20 for a loss.

There was also a system of bonus payments designed as an incentive for me to attain representative honours. For a couple of 'caps' with the Cumbria side I was to receive £750 but, even more attractively, if I made the Great Britain side then I was in for even more handsome bonuses. My first GB cap would mean a payment of £10,000 from Carlisle and for my first overseas tour with the GB side I was to get £5,000. I was also to have access to a sponsored car, travelling expenses and, importantly for me, I would continue to be allowed to stay in Jedburgh. In total the deal was probably worth not much short of £200,000 over the five-year period until 1997. Kevin was happy with the deal that he was being offered and it really did look as if we would both be enlisting with the paid ranks.

Carlisle were also recruiting in Hawick at the time — my cousin Colin Paxton was one of three Hawick boys who agreed terms — and the arrangement was that we would all travel down together for training and match days.

It was looking good. I would be with a bunch of lads that I knew. I would be making some decent money and I could have the best of both worlds by not giving up the life in Jed that meant so much to me. So what went wrong?

While the negotiations were going on we had the family lawyer overseeing our interests. He ran the financial rule over the club and wasn't particularly happy with what he found. In particular, he discovered that their accounts for 1989 showed them to be technically insolvent. This caused us all some concern. Their investment in me represented a huge outlay for them and we began to wonder if they could really afford it. Our lawyer and the club became involved in correspondence and the club assured him that the insolvency was nothing out of the ordinary for all but the top professional clubs. They assured him that the club's borrowings were secured against directors' professional guarantees and because these directors were 'men of substance' there was no problem on that front. The club chairman also told our lawyer that, in any case, my recruitment was to be supported by 'a separate sponsorship arrangement with a nationally known company'.

I've no doubt that all of this was true. However, at the back of my mind was the niggling doubt that if I signed professional forms then, to all intents and purposes, I became just a piece of meat which could be sold on the open market to the highest bidder. I knew that I still had a lot of good rugby in me and — keeping in mind that I'd already had approaches from top-flight Rugby League clubs — I was worried that, perfectly understandably, Carlisle might want to sell me on for a profit at some point in the future. This would have meant moving further south and out of Jedburgh. It was a prospect that I didn't relish one little bit.

Eventually the whole affair just dwindled and died. Carlisle were probably put off by the lawyer's letters and they must have lost interest because the negotiations stopped and their plans came to nothing.

In retrospect I'm glad. I know that my heart was never in it — Carlisle probably suspected that as well — and I still had some good times to come with my club and Scotland. The attraction for me was that I could have earned decent money playing rugby, albeit League, and all the while I could have remained in Jedburgh.

Soon after the Carlisle deal had fallen through Sheffield Eagles were on my doorstep looking for a signature. They were offering the same kind of money but, after the Carlisle deal had bitten the dust, I'd finally made up my mind that League wasn't for me. I met their coach in Jedburgh and he telephoned me the following week but my answer was no.

As I've said earlier, there is still a great divide between Union and League but in light of the great upheaval which Union is undergoing at the time of writing, I don't know how much longer this divide will prevail. The 'amateur' game kind of looks down its nose at League but I have to admit that losing my amateur status wasn't something which particularly bothered me. Alan Tait comes back to his native Kelso whenever he can each summer. He still gets on well with the Kelso folk and is just as welcome at Poynder Park as he was before he signed professional forms. Borderers don't look upon crossing the great divide between Union and League as an act of betrayal. For those working-class Border players who are good enough it represents an opportunity to earn a good wage and to accumulate cash for themselves and their families for later life. In the Borders I don't think that anybody begrudges them that.

I've no regrets. So far as Carlisle was concerned the decision was made for me because they never got back in touch. But, in view of the approaches that I've had from them and Sheffield Eagles, from Alan Tait and from other League scouts, there's no question that if I had wanted to go over to League then I could have done so. Probably, too, I could have done quite well and made myself and the family a pile of cash. But, as I've always said, there's more to life than money and although I'll now never know what might have been within the professional ranks it's not something which I'll lose a moment's sleep over. I'm happy with my lot in life and it seems to me that that's a blessing not given to many folks these days.

So far as cash and the Union game is concerned I have to congratulate myself on my foresight because — and this was written before the International Board finally got around to ending the hypocrisy of 'shamateurism' — I have no doubt that before very much longer there will be an élite group of players at the top of the game who are, to all intents and purposes, professionals. It was already happening in many countries. I know from personal experience just how much it takes to be an international player. Even since the time that I was first involved in the late Eighties the demands made upon the players' time have spiralled almost out of control. It will soon become impossible for an international player to hold down a proper day-to-day job. If you're not equipped for the public relations or marketing business and are working in an ordinary occupation then employers don't get the kind of glad-handing spin-off which providing a job for a rugby internationalist traditionally provides. In other words if, like me, the internationalist of the future is a lorry driver then he is not going to have time to work for his employer and 'work' for his international manager and coaches. I've been lucky with my bosses. They've been interested in rugby and they've been understanding to a fault when it came to the time off work that has been required to recover from my injuries. But even in my time it has become almost impossible to satisfy the requirements of work, family and international rugby.

The situation will get worse. Worldwide the game of rugby is on a roller-coaster and unless one of the major rugby nations shouts stop then it is going to go careering faster and faster until the game has to become fully professional at international level and throughout the summer of 1995 that seemed to be the route the game was following.

There is no sign that New Zealand, Australia or South Africa for that matter, are willing to admit that too many demands are being made of their top players and so, I guess, that if the rest of the world wants to compete with the Southern Hemisphere nations on an equal basis then we will have to follow their lead and our players will, effectively, become full-time rugby professionals. I've spoken to very few of the top players who actually want to be paid for playing rugby. Mostly, they just want to be recompensed for the huge amounts of time that training and all the rest of it means away from family and work and that sounds to me very much like the 'broken time payments' which caused the rift between Union and League in the first place.

International Rugby Union is now a multi-million pound business and probably before the end of the century the top players will be full-time professionals who are paid for playing for their clubs and countries and as 1995 drew to a close most of the world's rugby administrators were acknowledging that fact.

I look at the New Zealanders who played for Italian clubs during their close season at home. Why were they there? I know that they were there because they were making a good living from the game and I'm not just talking about board and beer money. These Southern Hemisphere players who spent 12 months of the year playing rugby were professionals and yet they were allowed to play for their national sides and compete, as amateurs, against us. It was appalling hypocrisy but for too long the authorities just turned a blind eye.

This was not just fanciful hearsay. I know that in New Zealand players were being paid. In 1990 when Scotland went to New Zealand as Grand Slam champions I was approached by a guy not literally waving his cheque book, but as near as dammit. He wanted me to play for Taranaki, one of NZ's top teams. He was going to give me a car, a 'job', spending money, accommodation and, into the bargain, he was going to fly the family out. It was the end of a hard tour and I wasn't interested so it didn't go any further but that was concrete proof of how the game operated in the Southern Hemisphere.

Basically the game is trapped. It can't survive without the big sponsorship deals that it's now involved in and, in many cases, the sponsors are calling the tune. At the World Cup in 1991, for instance, and again in 1995, we had the crazy experience of the players and the ref standing waiting until a TV man at the side of the pitch had given him the thumbs-up for the kick-off. We weren't allowed to start until the adverts had finished on ITV! That's what the game is coming to and whether we like it or not TV and big-time sponsors will run rugby in the future. As players we just looked at the millions of pounds that our efforts brought in and we wondered whether we shouldn't have a share.

When rugby was truly amateur in the sense that it was totally self-supporting and hadn't sold out to commercialism then the ruling bodies could stand on the high moral ground and tell the players that they had to be lily-white amateurs. Fair enough. But those responsible for the well-being of the game allowed it to become professionalised therefore they didn't any longer have a strong moral case when they were telling the players what they could and couldn't do.

In Scotland the international players now have a trust fund which is managed by representatives of the squad and Murrayfield officials. It works well but nobody is going to get rich on the proceeds. The players also have an official agent, the former Scotland captain Ian McLauchlan, and he does a lot of good work on the players' behalf signing deals for attendances at functions and the like.

Currently — and it may be 'all change' if the IB decides to embrace professionalism as it should — the set-up is that if a player is paid a fee for attending a function, for instance, then 20 per cent of the fee goes into the players' pool and the remainder is for his own use. Obviously, if you want to put yourself about a bit then you can make a bit of money. Some players are keen and others aren't. But nobody is getting rich. The World Cup in 1991 was the time when we could have made some real money but we were stymied by the Scottish Rugby Union who saw control of the players passing out of their hands. As a team we were riding on the crest of a wave after the Grand Slam the year before and commercial organisations were queuing up to be associated with a winning 'product'. As a squad we had appointed our own agents and they were busy on our behalf. They put together some big money deals, including one with a major Scottish brewery. Unfortunately, it wasn't the brewery with which the SRU already had a substantial deal and it was torpedoed by Murrayfield. That caused a great deal of ill feeling within the squad. The skipper, David Sole, as the players' spokesman, was in the forefront of the discussions with the Union and a lot of personal animosity was generated as a result. I think this whole affair accelerated David's early retirement which was a great loss for the Scottish game. At the end of the World Cup in which we had finished fourth, and which had generated millions of pounds in revenue, I received the princely sum of £368.

Now some will say that it is sufficient that you should play for your country for honour alone. Of course it's an honour to play for Scotland but it wasn't the players who started the commercial ball rolling. It was the rugby authorities. It wasn't the players who decided that there would be squad sessions on virtually every Sunday in the season. It was the rugby authorities. We have really just become pawns in a huge and costly game and the stage will be reached soon when players will have to make the choice between family, careers and playing for their country. The alternatives are to pay international players sufficiently well so that the choice between self, family and country doesn't have to be made, or to turn back the clock and restore the game to the true amateur sport that it used to be when international players just turned up on the morning of the match and let their natural rugby talent take care of proceedings in the afternoon. The time is fast approaching when the authorities will no longer be able to have it both ways, a state of affairs which, at the time of writing, was being belatedly acknowledged. For too long players had been caught in the middle and it was only a matter of time before somthing had to give.

That, as I see it, is the big picture. On a personal level I want to say that the SRU have never been less than generous to me. I've had a couple of serious injuries which have kept me off my work for over six months in total. On both occasions the Union have stepped in with assistance from the Injured Players' Trust Fund either by topping up my wage to account for the overtime that I was losing through not working or, as was the case in the injury I suffered at the end of 1994, by reimbursing my employers who generously continued to pay my salary while I was on the mend for 14 weeks. Put in simple terms this has meant that my family haven't gone hungry while I've not been earning. I'd like to see the existence of this fund made more widely known and I'd like to see club players benefit from it more as well.

One thing which always tended to stick in my craw, though, was the number of SRU committee men who would tag along whenever we went abroad. Take Dublin for instance. Whenever we went across there to play the Irish the plane would carry the 21 players, the coaches, the selectors and the management. Fair enough. But then you would have a couple of dozen 'buffties' and, often enough, their wives who were just along for the trip. Their toughest task of the weekend was making sure that their golf clubs were on board so that they could get away for a round of golf while the rest of us were slogging our guts out on the training field. Goodness knows what it must cost the SRU to mount an expedition like that. The 'buffties' would no doubt argue that the trip is their reward for the work that they put in but it's always seemed to me to be way over the top and I'm sure that the money it cost would be better spent elsewhere for the good of the game. Some of them, I'm sure, are just delighted to be on board the gravy train. I don't know how they can do it.

When I was out injured during 1994 I was invited along to be with the squad for the French match at Murrayfield. It was a nice gesture to be asked along but I would never do it again. I just felt so out of place. You weren't actually part of the playing side and I just felt like a hanger-on. That's how most of these 'buffties' must feel all the time. It's not for me and when my playing days are over then if I'm not involved in coaching or helping Jed out in some other way then I'll just pay at the gate the same as everyone else.

As I write, the game in Scotland is about to undergo a transformation with élite, eight-team divisions heading up the club structure. I can see a situation developing where, with the top players concentrated on just a handful of clubs, commercial sponsorship will be sucked in by these élite clubs to the detriment of the rest. We tend to forget when we're talking about the international side and the top clubs that they represent just the tip of the pyramid. To most rugby people the game is about their own, maybe small, unfashionable club and the second, third and fourth XVs. There's a very real danger that with the marketing focus on the élite teams at the top these minnows of the game might shrivel and die. If you don't fertilise the grassroots of the game then pretty soon you won't have a game to speak of.

Undoubtedly, with the streamlined élite club structure and even talk of a European championship, a lot of sponsorship money is going to be attracted to the game and I just hope that the SRU will make sure that a lot of the cash is redistributed around the less fashionable areas of the game so that we still have young players coming into the system at the bottom because without them, in no time at all, we won't have senior players of sufficient quality and quantity coming out at the other end.

I've been lucky. I have always looked upon rugby as a hobby, and still do. Sure, I would have liked to have made a bit of money from the game, and if I can in the future then I certainly won't be complaining, but it was never a motivating factor for me.

The momentous decision by the International Board during the late summer of 1995 that the game is to turn professional now means that there will be almost unlimited opportunities to earn money from the game. How much, and where the money is to come from, remain the two big unanswered questions. There are still some tough decisions to be made and common sense will have to prevail on all sides.

However, playing for Scotland was a boyhood dream and it came true. I used to dream about a Lions tour and I did that too. I've seen parts of the world that I never would have done if it hadn't been for rugby. I've given the game a lot and it has cost me a lot in terms of pain and, at times even despair, but I got the best out of the deal and if I had my time over again I wouldn't change a thing.

CHAPTER 9

EMERGENCY WARD NINE

The Medics and Me

IT WAS the noise it made which more than anything else persuaded me that this was more than just a routine training injury. It sounded like a rifle shot and it preceded the most excruciating pain by just a second or two. The whole episode seemed to be taking place in slow motion. I was running. I was passing and, simultaneously, I was tackled. My left foot remained anchored to the ground and the knee was twisted around to the right. Before I had even hit the ground I knew that it was bad; within a couple of hours I knew that it would put me on the sidelines for some time and within a couple of weeks I knew that it meant my international career was hanging in the balance.

It was Thursday, 25 August 1994, three days before the annual Selkirk seven-a-side tournament. With my Jed clubmates I had started training earlier than usual. The forthcoming season was an important one for Scottish club rugby. It was to be the last with the 14-team divisions. In 1995–96 only eight clubs would be in the top divisions therefore it was essential that we gave it our best shot if Jed were to claim a place among the élite. Accordingly, I had never felt fitter by the time the start-of-season seven-a-sides came around. I had recovered from the hand injury which brought my international comeback season to a premature halt and I was raring to go.

We were limbering up for the Selkirk tournament. It was a fine evening and all seemed right with the world. The Jed coaches, Donald Miller and Robbie Lindores, said we would 'do' some sevens practice. They asked if we wanted a proper game or if we wanted to run through some moves with an 'unopposed' session. I said that 'unopposed' rugby was a waste of time and that we should have a proper game. Me and my big mouth!

We split into two seven-a-side teams and everything was going well. I had injured a shoulder in a tackle and I must have pinched a nerve because the arm had gone 'dead'. However, the feeling soon returned and I got back into the fray with a vengeance. It was the second half and I made a break just as I had done thousands of times before. I got to the opposition 22 with just Chris Richards to beat. I drew our young full-back towards me, committing him to the tackle. As I did so I heard brother Kevin shout for the pass. I looked over my right shoulder to focus for the transfer and as I did so Chris moved in to tackle me, also from the right.

It was pre-season and the Riverside Park grass was still pretty long. At the same time I was wearing new boots with moulded soles. The sequence of events which followed replay in my mind like slow motion. Chris lined me up for the tackle. I was looking over my shoulder, shaping up to pass. It seemed like a straightforward situation, the kind of situation that I had experienced many times before. But then my foot got stuck in the ground. Whether it was due to the new boots or the long grass, or a combination of both, I don't know but as Chris went through with the tackle I recall thinking 'something's going to happen here. I can't get my foot out of the ground'.

The weight of the tackle twisted me around but with my left foot anchored to the ground something had to give and, unfortunately, the 'thing' which gave was my knee. The whole thing seemed to be taking place in slow motion. There was the most almighty crack from my leg and I thought initially that it had been broken. The pain was excruciating and I let out an almighty shriek as I fell to the ground. Still, the whole thing

Mini rugby at Jed: the start of something big.

*Five Nations' debut against Wales at Murrayfield: it wasn't a try this time
but we still won 23–7.*

The Grand Slammers: Scotland's line-up in the winners-take-all match against England in March, 1990.

Exit, stage right, despite the efforts of opposite number Richard Hill in the 1990 Grand Slam show-down at Murrayfield.

Keep them guessing: Rob Andrew and Rory Underwood aren't too sure what comes next. Murrayfield, 17 March 1990.

The sweet taste of success: Grand Slam champers for Tony Stanger, Scott Hastings and me.

The Border League, the world's oldest rugby competition, and here Jed are in action against near neighbours but old rivals Kelso.

The best of enemies: 'Chic' Chalmers and I grew up together with Scotland but the boot's on the other foot when it's Jed-Forest v Melrose.

Combined Scottish Districts against Auckland at Mansfield Park: the game marked my return to the scrum-half berth.

Brothers in arms: Robert Jones, my British Lions' scrum-half rival and mate, photographed in front of one of the world's best known landmarks. Sydney Harbour Bridge, 1989.

So...

Near...

Yet...

So Far! My comeback game for Scotland against England in 1994. Jon Hall drags me down inches short of the line. England won with the last kick of the game. We were all shattered and Gav did a 'Gazza' on nationwide TV.

*Man at work: it's not all goals and glamour on the international stage.
In the cab of my Mainetti truck.*

The Armstrong clan: Shona, Nicole, Darren and me.

seemed to be happening out of real time and it took an age before I hit the ground. It was almost as if this was happening to someone else and I was just a bystander.

Once I was on the ground, though, the reality of the situation hit me. I was in the most awful pain. Everybody was crowding around me. Kevin was there and I grabbed hold of him. In fact I was in so much pain and gripped his shirt so tightly that I almost ripped it off his back. An ambulance was called and I was carried into the dressing-room. The pain had eased slightly but each time I tried to straighten the leg it came back, worse than before. The ambulancemen gave me some gas which also acted as a painkiller and made things a wee bit better. They put my leg into a splint but when the knee joint was straightened the pain was so bad that I almost passed out. I asked them to loosen the splint and they did. The ambulance took me the 15 miles to the Borders General Hospital and I was wheeled into the casualty department.

By the time I arrived at the hospital Roy Laidlaw, who had been at Riverside and had seen what had happened, had already been on the telephone to Donald Macleod, the Scottish Rugby Union's top medical man. Donald had phoned the BGH and had spoken to the young doctor who was on duty at the casualty department. The young medic knew to expect me and he found himself in the situation of having to report not only to his own boss but also to Donald.

The knee was examined and X-rayed and the diagnosis was that I had twisted the joint and pulled a calf muscle. However, I was the one who was suffering the pain and I reckoned that it was more serious than that. Two years beforehand I had 'done in' the medial ligaments on the same knee and this injury felt worse than that one had done. I was a bit of an expert in rugby injuries and was certainly an expert when it came to the pain! When I got home that night I telephoned Donald Macleod and told him that I wasn't really happy with the diagnosis and that I felt it was more serious than the medics at BGH thought.

Donald agreed and made arrangements to get me into the Princess Margaret Rose orthopaedic hospital in Edinburgh after the weekend. I went up to see Dr Richard Nutton on the Monday and he carried out his own investigation. From his initial examination he reckoned that the cruciate ligament might have snapped or that, at best, there was severe cartilage damage. He warned me to expect the worst and said that he would try to have me admitted to hospital the following day when they would put a probe into the knee and get a good look at the damage. I was driven back up to Edinburgh the next day and had the knee examined under a general anaesthetic. I came round about midday and Dr Nutton was standing by the bed. He didn't pull any punches and I didn't want him to. He told me that the damage to the knee was about as bad as it could get. I had done the anterior cruciate ligament completely and the medial ligament had stretched and loosened. Two cartilages had been torn and only the cartilage coming off the bone had prevented the medial ligaments from snapping in two. It was a right old mess. The ligaments and cartilages basically hold the joint together and because of the twisting motion that the joint had suffered in the tackle they had all just snapped or stretched like oversize elastic bands.

Dr Nutton said that I would be out of the game for at least a year. He had prepared me for the worst and so it didn't come as quite the shock that it might have done. Nevertheless, as I lay there in that bed I couldn't help thinking, just occasionally, why me? Dr Nutton said the lateral ligament was the only part of the knee that wasn't damaged but, even so, everything could be fixed. It would mean a total reconstruction of the joint and it would take time but it could be put back together again.

He said that it would take several weeks for the swelling from the initial injury to settle down after which they could begin work in earnest. However, he said that when they had been inside the joint with the optic-fibre probe they had trimmed up the cruciate ligament and all the cartilages. I was still pretty groggy from the anaesthetic at this stage and still coming to terms with the news that I would be out of the game for 12 months at least. I hadn't even had a chance to tell Shona what the verdict was before the phone started ringing at home in Jedburgh. Seemingly the SRU had released a statement that the news was bad and that I was going to be on the sidelines for a long time. It was, maybe, just a breakdown in communication but I was angry that Shona had got the verdict from the newspapers and not from me.

Once the enormity of the injury had sunk in I began to feel really depressed. I had been feeling fitter than I had felt in a long time and I had been particularly looking forward to playing against South Africa at the start of the 1994–95 season. I had never played against the Springboks and it was a contest which I had relished.

On 11 October, six weeks after the initial injury, I had the operation to replace the cruciate ligament. It was rebuilt using carbon fibres and a strip from my patella tendon.

The carbon fibres are the same stuff that they make Formula One racing cars from so that should be more than up to the job. What followed next was, in many ways, more difficult to handle than the injury itself and the news that I would be out of the game for a year.

After the successful operation I had to undergo months of physiotherapy. I was driven up to Edinburgh for physiotherapy thrice a week and on Tuesdays and Thursdays I strengthened the knee on the weights at Riverside Park. It seemed like a never-ending series of medical appointments and intensive physiotherapy. Who says international sportsmen lead glamorous lives?

I was off work for four-and-a-half months and here I was immensely grateful to the Scottish Rugby Union because I benefited from their injured players' fund. My wages were reimbursed to my long-suffering employer Mainetti (UK) in Jedburgh. Also, as befits my father's line of work in the insurance business, I had personal injury insurance. I didn't suffer financially as a result of not working but it could have been so different if the SRU hadn't acted as they did or if I hadn't taken out insurance of my own. I'd strongly advise any young player to get along to their friendly local insurance man and arrange cover which includes rugby injuries. Don't think it can't happen to you. It can and it probably will.

Over the years I've provided more work for the medics than I care to remember. Probably, the injuries that I've picked up have been due to my style of play. I tend to get stuck in but, playing sometimes almost as an auxiliary wing-forward I tend to get stuck in against players who are at least six inches taller and three stones or more heavier. I'm 5'8" and 13½st and I don't think I'm a shrinking violet. In fact I think that you are much more likely to get hurt if you hold back. But, even so, don't believe all that stuff that folk tell you about the bigger they are the harder they fall. In international rugby in particular, these 6'7" giants weighing in at 17 or 18 stones aren't just there for show. They really do punch their weight and that 18 stones is made up of bone, gristle and muscle. If you are going to mix it with these guys then your technique has to be spot on otherwise you're going to get hurt.

I think that in my rugby career maybe I've brought a lot of the injuries that I've suffered upon myself. I was taught from the mini-rugby days, that if you were a scrum-half then you didn't pass on dud ball to your fly-half. That was a truism which stayed with me throughout my playing days and, as a result, if our forwards were shovelling back crap from the lineouts or if delivery from rucks and mauls didn't live up to Bill McLaren's famed 'chocolate bar from a slot-machine service' then I held on to the ball and took the hidings that were coming my way. If I hadn't then I was just passing trouble down the line. In this way I always tried to protect my fly-halves. Ask 'Chic' Chalmers. I'm sure he would agree! I'm no softy and, to be truthful, I really enjoyed the rough-and-tumble aspect of the game, even at international level, but over the years all those poundings begin to take their toll.

Until I started playing for Scotland in 1988 I really hadn't suffered any injuries to speak of. But during the Grand Slam season in 1990 I began to suffer trouble with my left elbow. Some cartilage and flakes of bone had become dislodged and they had calcified within the joint. I had an operation in the summer of 1990 and, touch wood, I've not been troubled with the elbow since.

Which is not to say that other parts of my anatomy have not rebelled against the treatment they have received over the years.

Just before the start of the 1992 Five Nations campaign I was playing for Jed against Currie at Riverside Park. I had just kicked the ball into the air. My right leg was off the ground and my left foot was still fixed to the turf when Currie's open-side flanker Alan Elms arrived on the scene like an Exocet missile. I was knocked up in the air. I felt the left knee go and the result was a three-quarter tear in the medial ligament. It wasn't Elms's fault. It was just one of those things but I was to be out of the game for three months and I missed the entire Five Nations Championship.

I was back and raring to go the following season but in the opening match of the 1993 Five Nations tournament, against Ireland at Murrayfield, I was in the wars again. This was an injury which didn't amount to much at the time but one which would have serious, and for me heartbreaking, consequences.

We beat the Irish 15–3 in pretty convincing fashion but in the course of the 80 minutes I had suffered a groin injury. It happened when I bent down to pick up a wayward ball and first one and then another Irishman descended upon me. I did the splits and knew right away that a muscle had been torn. I struggled through the Five Nations with the aid of ultrasound treatment but by the end of the season the pain wasn't really easing. It was so bad that some mornings I could hardly get out of bed.

At the same time the race was on to get fit for the British Lions tour to New Zealand that summer. Despite what many journalists wrote at the time, I was really desperate to go on that trip. Unlike the 1989 tour to Australia when I played second-fiddle to my old mate Robert Jones, I would have gone to New Zealand as first-choice scrum-half — coach Ian McGeecham apparently said later that my name was the first on the team sheet

— and it would have been a superb way in which to bring the curtain down on my career.

The groin, though, was causing very real problems. I made things worse by training with Jed in an effort to get into the seven to play at Melrose Sports. I like the Border seven-a-side circuit and Melrose is the blue riband of the abbreviated game. Stupidly, in hindsight, I really pushed myself in an effort to get into the Jed side for the Greenyards tournament.

Eventually Donald Macleod said that the only way I was going to be in with a shout of getting on that plane for New Zealand was if I agreed to have a cortisone injection straight into the damaged area of the groin. I drove up to see Mr Macleod at St John's Hospital, Livingston, where he works, and he administered the 'jag'. I thought that it had worked right away because for the first time in months I was free of pain.

Unfortunately, though, Donald explained that he'd put a touch of local anaesthetic in with the cortisone and it was the painkiller which had led to the instant 'cure'. The cortisone treatment was definitely working but, sadly, it didn't work in time.

We were due to travel down to London for a training session with the Lions but I had to call off with the explanation that Mr Macleod had said that the treatment had to be given time to work. In the meantime, he had said, I should be excused training.

Four days later Geoff Cooke from the Lions management team telephoned me with the news that I was out. I was absolutely gutted. That night I telephoned my dad, almost in tears, and told him that I was out. At first he didn't know what I was talking about but eventually I was able to tell him that the Lions management had been in touch and they had told me that I was out of the tour party. It came as a severe blow to my mum and dad as well because they were booked up to go on a supporters' tour.

As Rabbie Burns put it, 'the best laid schemes of mice and men gang aft agley'. These plans had certainly 'gang agley' and then some. My plan had been to go to New Zealand and then to retire from international rugby as the world's number one scrum-half. That may seem immodest, and maybe lots of people will consider it to be out of character, but on the rugby field I have always had self-belief. I have played against the best in the world and, once I was into the swing of international rugby, I always felt I was better than they were. You have to have an arrogant self-belief when you're playing at the top. You don't have to shout it from the roof tops but you have to know, within yourself, that you're as good and better than anybody else. Once you begin to doubt your own abilities then, at international level, you're finished.

We had two young kids at the time and Shona wasn't that keen for me to fly off to the other side of the world but she understood why I wanted to do it and she understood my bitter disappointment when it didn't happen. Mum and Dad continued with their trip but it had to be cut short when, just two weeks into the tour, my grandad died suddenly. They came home for the funeral and if I had been there I would have come home too. We are a very close family and I wouldn't have felt like going back to New Zealand to resume the tour. Fortunately, as things turned out, I was at home and not 12,000 miles away on the other side of the world when I got a phone call telling me that my grandfather was having trouble with his heart. I was there when he died in intensive care. It meant so much to me to be at his side when he passed away. When things like that happen it helps you to get rugby into perspective. My grandad meant so much to me. I had stayed with him for seven years when I had returned to Jed as a teenager from Dunfermline and we had gone on holidays together since I was a toddler. We were very, very close and, with hindsight, the fact that I had been forced to drop out of the tour looks now as if it was a blessing in disguise but that wasn't how it had appeared in the early summer of 1993.

Throughout that summer I was at a very low ebb. I had missed the Lions tour, my grandfather had died and I was feeling pretty dispirited. As the summer wore on and the groin injury eventually began to clear up I felt that I needed a fresh challenge.

I was jaded and in desperate need of the change which, they say, is as good as a rest.

So far as I was concerned the 'change' most needed was a sabbatical away from the scrum-half berth. I talked it over with my family and then wrote to the SRU telling them that I needed a fresh challenge and that I was going to try playing somewhere other than scrum-half. Maybe I was naïve and maybe it was the wrong decision but at the time that was how I felt and that was what I wanted to do.

As the summer progressed the groin injury cleared up and I got into training for the start of the 1993–94 season. The training was going well and, psychologically, I felt that a huge burden had been lifted from my shoulders. Soon, though, I came under all sorts of pressure to get back to the scrum-half slot. Jed were struggling in the Scottish league and we were even in the relegation zone for a while. Grant Farquharson had taken over at scrum-half at Riverside Park and I was playing at stand-off, centre and full-back. I never really got the chance to settle down in any one position. Eventually, the Jed selectors decided that they were going to drop Grant and they told me that if I didn't move back to scrum-half then they would play someone else there. I felt sorry for Grant, whom I've known since we were youngsters together, but I felt a responsibility to the club.

While all of this was happening I was approached by the Scottish Combined Districts selectors with a request that I turn out for them at scrum-half against Auckland who were touring Scotland at the same time as the All Blacks. I agreed and was almost immediately glad that I had. It went OK and I really enjoyed it. It took ten minutes for me to get back into the swing of things but after that I felt like I had never been away.

That was the first time I had played scrum-half since my decision to seek fresh pastures and it seemed as if there were a number of forces conspiring to get me to change my mind.

I watched Scotland surrendering 51–15 to the All Blacks at Murrayfield. Even sitting in the stand I really felt the pain of that defeat. It looked to me like the Scottish team were 'feart' of the

Kiwis and they gave them far too much respect. As I was leaving someone shouted from the crowd 'It's all your fault Gary Armstrong'. Maybe he was only kidding but, whoever he was, he certainly got me to thinking. You're Scottish through and through and, even if you're not playing, you don't like to see Scotland howked like they were that black November day at Murrayfield. So when the next stage of the 'conspiracy' to get me back into the number nine shirt unfolded I was in a much better frame of mind and much more likely to say yes.

Mickey Steele-Bodger, of the Barbarians, telephoned asking if I would be available for selection — at scrum-half — for the Baa-Baas side which was to meet the All Blacks in Cardiff. I said that I would be and a little later he called me back to say that I was in the side. The other Scots in the Invitation XV were Scott Hastings, who was skipper, and Rob Wainwright. It was a good side and I was sure that we could give the Kiwis a run for their money. As it was, we went down but I think we gave a good account of ourselves.

Personally, though, the game meant that I would be re-acquainting myself with the medics. I had been really enjoying myself and was relishing the reality of playing in front of big crowds again. Then, about 15 minutes into the second half, I sprung a rib cartilage. I tried to ignore it but every time I was tackled the cartilage would pop out. It was getting pretty sore and so I had to call it a day. I'd just come back from the groin injury and before that I'd lost a season with the knee and when this happened at Cardiff I have to admit that, for a fleeting second or two, I began to wonder if it was all worth it.

That was me until after Christmas. I was out for five weeks and made my comeback for Jed against Langholm on the day that Scotland lost their 1994 Five Nations opener against Wales in Cardiff. Scotland lost badly, 26–6, and I watched the game on telly. The boys hadn't seemed to have any 'go' about them and then, in the last minute of the game, Andy Nicol, the Dundee HSFP scrum-half, damaged his ribs and that was him out for the season.

Scotland were now up against it, both generally speaking and, specifically, so far as filling the number 9 shirt was concerned.

I wasn't expecting the call but, when I had made my decision about seeking a fresh challenge, I had assured the Scottish team manager Dunc Paterson that in an emergency he could give me a call. This wasn't arrogance on my part — or at least I hope it wasn't — it was just that Duncie had said that he would respect my decision if I would agree to go back to the scrum-half berth if the going got tough.

Duncie phoned me at work but I wasn't there. My boss, Alistair McIntosh, took the call from Dunc because I was out on the road. When Alistair, who's a Dundee HSFP man, told me what Duncan wanted I said that I wasn't nearly fit enough to play international rugby. Alistair said not to worry about that and that he would give me the time off to get fit. Duncie telephoned that night and it all happened from there. He offered me my old place back and said that I had three weeks in which to get fit enough to face the English at Murrayfield. With my Border Reiver roots I didn't need much incentive to have a real crack at the Auld Enemy.

For the next three weeks Alistair gave me every afternoon off and I spent the time at Riverside Park with the Jed trainer 'Chico' Woods. I did a lot of weights in the gym plus sprint work and built up my stamina by means of a two-stone weights jacket.

For public consumption, the team to play in the Calcutta Cup match was published with an AN Other in the number 9 slot. I had to prove my fitness in Jed's game against Gala two weeks before the international. I suppose that in reality I was in the side — and the media never made any secret of it — but, as much for my own benefit as anybody else's, I wanted to prove to myself that I was still up to the task.

Once it became known that I was back in the Scotland side I was touched by all of the things that people said and wrote about me. It didn't really add to the pressure because I tend to take these kind of things in my stride but some of the comment was away over the top and made me out to be some kind of superman.

On the day against England I felt really good. If anything, maybe I had over-trained. I had still been doing weights until the Wednesday before the squad got together in Edinburgh. It was a game which we should have won. We lost 15–14 when Jonathan Callard put over a disputed penalty with, literally, the last kick of the game. That was really hard to take. It was a real sickener. We had all put a lot of effort into that game. The boys wanted to erase the memory of Cardiff and, more particularly, to show that we were better than that 51–15 defeat by the All Blacks had indicated.

Gavin Hastings took the defeat particularly badly. I was soaking in the bath when Gav came back to the dressing-room. He said that he'd 'done a Gazza' and nobody knew what the hell he was talking about. Eventually, though, he said that, just like the soccer-playing Geordie buffoon, he had burst into tears during the live TV interview. We all felt for him. A win in the new Murrayfield stadium would have meant so much to us all but especially to Gavin who, as skipper, had taken a lot of the flak for Scotland's disappointing performances up to then. I didn't enjoy an entirely incident-free return. I escaped with eight stitches in my left ear and finished the match with a head bandage so big that it looked like a turban. Nevertheless, I was glad to come away more or less in one piece. Next port of call on the Five Nations trail was Lansdowne Road where we were to take on the Irish.

Lansdowne Road in Dublin has never been my favourite international venue. There is just something about the place that I don't like. For one thing a railway line runs underneath one of the stands and the dressing-rooms seem to be deep underground. You can hear the trains passing overhead and you have to climb what seems like umpteen flights of stairs before you get out on to the pitch. Funnily enough, Lansdowne Road was my Jed mentor Roy Laidlaw's favourite ground. He scored his famous hat-trick of tries there and Laidlaw's corner is forever named in his honour. Maybe, that's another reason why I was never particularly happy there. I didn't like comparisons between me and Roy and maybe subconsciously I felt increased pressure to perform.

In any event, my misgivings about Dublin were about to be confirmed. It wasn't much of a game. The gale which howled down the pitch put paid to any chance that it might have had of being a classic. We drew 6–6 and at least it wasn't a defeat. But for me the Championship was over and — even if I didn't know it at the time, my international career was once again in doubt.

I can't for the life of me remember how it happened, but I came away from a ruck with a searing pain in my right hand. At first it just felt like a bad stave but the pain got worse and worse and, even with my catalogue of medical mishaps, it was the worst pain I have ever felt.

It was absolute murder. I went into hospital on the Monday following our return from Ireland and was operated on the next day. The surgeon reckoned that the thumb must have been bent back and twisted. The tendon was ripped off the bone. He said that it was an injury which was particularly common among skiers who come a cropper on artificial slopes. They get their thumbs hooked in the nylon surface and, hey presto, the result is the same as if you have come off second-best against a bunch of mad-dog Irishmen at Lansdowne Road. The surgeon said that the injury was so prevalent among skiers on the Pentland Hills artificial slopes on the outskirts of Edinburgh that within the medical trade they called it Hillend Thumb. That was the first time, though, that they had seen such an injury in a rugby player.

So that was it. With my Irish Hillend Thumb I was to be out for six weeks and my international comeback had been curtailed through injury. Over the summer the thumb healed to perfection and I just had the operation scar to remind me of my Lansdowne Road misadventure. Despite the problem with the hand I really had recovered my appetite for the game and I was determined to go out in a blaze of glory the following season.

I had wanted to make sure of my Scotland place and then to play just one more season at the top. Fate, though, had other ideas. An innocuous tackle in a seven-a-side practice match on my home turf put paid to all of that. That 6–6 draw on a storm-tossed Lansdowne Road, my least favourite international venue, was to be my last appearance in a Scotland shirt for the time being.

But I am determined that fate shall not have the last word. I want to retire from the international stage on my own terms and not having the timing of my Scotland farewell dictated by injury. I have played 30 times for Scotland and probably should have played half a dozen times more had not injuries intervened. I have fought back to fitness over the summer of 1995 and I intend to take the medics at their word when they tell me that, once mended, the damaged left knee should be as good as new.

I realise, probably better than most, just what it will take to win back my Scotland place but I am determined to give it a go. First of all I have to regain my place in the Jed team and then I have to summon up all my resources to mount one final push to get me back in the Scottish side. I know that I have the will-power to do it. I've had more than my share of hard knocks over the years but I've had lots of 'guid fun' along the way. It's the fun aspect in front of international crowds that drives me along. That, and a burning desire to play my last game for Scotland at a time and place of my own choosing. That's the target I've set myself. If I don't make it then at least I will have tried. To have gone out lame, and with a whimper, would have been much harder for me to live with. That wasn't the attitude of my Border forebears and it's not my attitude now. For at least one more Five Nations season I want to be able to say 'Jethart's Here!'

CHAPTER 10

FANTASY FOOTBALL

A Murrayfield Testimonial

THE SCENE is the new Murrayfield Stadium. It is a 67,500 sell-out and a World XV is taking on a Scotland Select. I have chosen both sides and have taken the liberty of selecting myself for the World XV. It's Rugby Union's first testimonial match and I am the lucky beneficiary. Fantasy football? Well, I can dream, can't I?

Nevertheless, let's have some fun by selecting the two sides which will entertain the huge Murrayfield crowd. The rules are that I must have played alongside or against those eligible for selection.

Let's start with full-back. There are only two contenders, Serge Blanco of France and Gavin Hastings of Scotland. These are the two best full-backs that I've ever seen in my time and it's a tough choice. However, it's going to be a case of au revoir Serge and hello Hastings. The full-back for my testimonial team is Andrew Gavin Hastings.

Scotland doesn't possess many world-class players but, without a doubt, Gavin comes into this category. Ever since he made his debut in 1986 he has had that swagger and confidence in his immense abilities which are infectious within a team. He went through a really bad patch after he was appointed Scotland captain but, with the 1993 British Lions in New Zealand and in the 1994–95 Five Nations Championship and the World Cup his leadership qualities, in addition to his personal play, shone through like a burning beacon. He had that rare ability to turn a game by a stroke of personal brilliance and there aren't many people you can say that about. But am I going to make him captain? I'm not sure. Let's look at the rest of the team and make a decision on that when the selection meeting is over.

My right winger is Ieaun Evans of Wales. I toured with Ieuan on the British Lions' trip to Australia in 1989 and I was impressed with everything he did. He is a 100 per cent trier and these are the kind of guys that I want in my side. He is deceptively pacy. By which I mean that he is a damned sight faster than he looks. He can also defend a bit and I'm more than happy to have him out on the right touchline.

I'm disregarding both Underwoods, Rory and Tony. The latter isn't half the player that his brother is and I just have a sneaking doubt about Rory's defence. Ireland's Simon Geoghegan also came into the reckoning. He's an exciting player with the ball in his hands but, again, I wonder about his defence and, also, I suspect that he isn't quite as good as he appeared to be when he first burst upon the international scene in 1991.

In the centre I'm picking Jeremy Guscott of England and to play inside him Philippe Sella of France. Guscott has come back, after long-term injury, to slot into England's 1995 Grand Slam side. Perhaps he isn't quite as sharp as he was beforehand but he's still a damned sight sharper than most. Guscott is one of those silky smooth players who seem to possess effortless pace. He can carve through a defence like a hot knife through butter and I'd rather play alongside him than against him.

Like Guscott, Sella is a class act. He's big and strong, immensely experienced and a hell of a good rugby player. He would be the perfect foil for Guscott. The Frenchman would have to take a crash course in the Jethart dialect but if he could manage that then he's in the side.

I had to make some pretty tough calls when I was choosing my centres. Giving the nod to Guscott and Sella meant that my

1990 Grand Slam team-mates Sean Lineen and Scott Hastings don't make the side. They certainly came into the reckoning along with Timmy Horan and Jason Little of Australia but I'm sticking with the Englishman and the Frenchman. I considered Will Carling for a moment or so but decided that he wasn't in the same class as Guscott or Sella or, as a duo, Scott or Sean. Apologies, though, to the two Scotsmen. Maybe they'll get into the Scottish side which will prove the opposition for my World XV!

On the left wing is the Great Entertainer himself, David Campese. Campo has thrilled rugby crowds all over the world. The game is now such big business that, whether we like it or not (and I do) we have a duty to entertain. When Murrayfield international tickets cost over 20 quid and those at Twickenham retail at more than 30 quid then, at those prices, crowds expect to be treated to a bit of a show. Campese fills that bill perfectly. He'll pull in the crowds at Murrayfield. He's been an outstanding player, maybe one of the best the game has ever seen.

Like many of those who get into my World XV, he has the capacity to alter his side's fortunes with a single act of breathtaking audacity. He can also lose games though, and he'll be told that we want no repeat of his throwaway goal-line pass which let Ieuan in to score and which helped the Lions to win the crucial third Test in 1989.

At stand-off I'm going to have Craig Chalmers. Now don't accuse me of favouritism. He's not just in the side because I'm playing scrum-half and I like him playing outside me. Chic is a much, much better player than his critics make him out to be. This is a class side I'm picking and I'm sure that with world-class players all around him we would have the opportunity to witness just how good Craig really is. He isn't just a kicking machine. He has a lot more to offer than that. It was a tragedy that Craig broke his arm in the 1993 Calcutta Cup game because I'm sure that if he had gone to New Zealand with the Lions then he would have blossomed and would have come back as the Home Unions' number one choice fly-half. Chic has a superb rugby brain. He has, too, great vision and I feel that we have never really seen the best of him in a Scotland shirt. He can kick, we all know that, but he also has a great break and his defence is better than most stand-offs that I have seen. Chic never shirks a tackle and that's not something that I could say about some fly-halves that I've played with and against.

There's been a lot of world-class fly-halves in my era. Grant Fox of New Zealand came into the reckoning for selection, as did Michael Lynagh of Australia but both, I believe, are out-and-out kicking machines. Rob Andrew of England is a great player but, as I see it, he doesn't use his backs as much as he should. The England packs behind which he has played have secured him fantastic possession over the years but, more often than not, he has kicked it away. With the likes of Guscott outside him I just wonder how good England could have been if Rob had made better use of the ball which has come his way. I want my World XV to put on a bit of a show with some scintillating running and so Fox, Lynagh and Andrew are discarded in favour of Craig. With Scotland maybe he hasn't had the benefit of the world-class players that the others have had around them and so has had to play to a pattern which best showed up the team's stengths. He'll show what he's really made of in my World XV.

I'm allowed to choose myself at scrum-half. It's my book after all! But if I wasn't in the team, or if I got injured, maybe I'd better have some replacements standing by. Rob Jones of Wales comes top of the list. He is a real class act. Rob has always been a bit of a role model for me. When I was capped at Under-18 level Rob got his first Welsh cap and I've always made a point of watching, and learning, from the things that Rob does on a rugby field. He has a tremendous service but possesses a devastating break as well. He's the best all-round scrum-half that I've seen during my time at the top.

Nick Farr-Jones of Australia also comes into the equation but Rob gets the nod before him. I discount, too, both Dewi Morris and Richard Hill of England. Again, like Rob Andrew, they have had the benefit of an armchair ride behind some colossal English packs but have never really shown that they deserved to be called world-class.

I have had a lot of trouble making up my mind about loose-head prop. I'm a great admirer of Ireland's Nick Popplewell but how could I discount my Grand Slam captain David Sole? There's probably not much to choose between them as scrummagers and they both get about the park in a way that no self-respecting prop should. Popplewell is fresher in the memory because he is still playing. Soley retired in 1992 — far too early but he had his reasons — but he remains one of the best players that I've ever seen or played alongside. Off the field he was a quietly spoken gent but once he was in a rugby shirt he became like a man possessed. I don't think I've played alongside anybody, except perhaps Fin Calder, who was so ruthlessly dedicated to the Scotland cause. Sole took no prisoners and he is my man in the number 1 shirt.

My hooker is the New Zealand captain Sean Fitzpatrick. He is a very fine hooker but also has a kind of aura about him. Or at least I thought so. When we played against him in 1990 and, later, in the 1991 World Cup third-place play-off in Cardiff, he impressed me with his authority and his control of the All Black side. It takes a big man to exert that kind of authority and Fitzpatrick seemed to manage it without any trouble. I think I might have to make him captain. The other candidates have to be Hastings and Sole. I'll have to think about that one.

Kenny Milne also came into the frame for the hooker's berth. Again, like Craig, Kenny is a much underrated player. He is a grafter and a big man for a hooker and, I'm certain, that if he had more self-belief then he would have been a genuinely world-class player. He has all the physical attributes necessary to become one but he just lacks that slight edge which self-belief gives you. Kenny is a much, much better player than John Allan who took his place during the 1991 World Cup before vanishing back to South Africa where he enlisted with the Springboks. I've played alongside both of them and there's no doubt that Kenny was the better player. However, Allan psyched him out in 1991.

There are some players who respond to the pressure of a rival breathing down their neck by upping the standard of their game. Others just get so worried about the prospect that their play suffers as a result. This is what happened to Kenny. If he had had more self-belief and had claimed his position with the firm statement on the playing field that he was the Scottish hooker and nobody, but nobody, was getting his place, then Allan wouldn't have got a single Scottish cap and he would have been back in South Africa long before he was.

England's Brian Moore didn't come within a mile of selection. I don't care that he had been first-choice hooker on two Lions' tours and has been top-dog for England in three Grand Slams, I'm afraid he just rubs me up the wrong way and he doesn't get into the side. He's a good player but there's no point in beating about the bush, I just can't stand him. He has got the biggest mouth in world rugby. How the RFU lets him get away with it I don't know. His comments after the 1995 Grand Slam game against Scotland when he went on telly right afterwards to lambast Scotland were pathetic. A bad loser is one thing but a sore winner is something else entirely. No doubt Moore will love the notoriety but I wouldn't like to be in his shoes the next time he comes to Murrayfield. There will, undoubtedly, be a target on his back. So, and no apologies Brian, you don't make the World XV.

The other prop is the All Black Richard Loe. OK, as his disciplinary record shows, he has a tendency to be a bit of a thug, but he'd be a good guy to have on your side. He's a hard, aggressive player who maybe goes over the score now and again but, in the rough and tumble of international rugby, you quite often need a guy like Loe in the side. He's the kind of bloke who makes the opposition think twice before taking any liberties. Loe did a lot of damage against us in the loose when we toured New Zealand in 1990. He was never too particular about where he placed his feet in the rucks — and I've still got the scars to prove it — but he really impressed me as a world-class prop forward and he is the man who fills my number 3 jersey.

If I was choosing my tight-head prop on scrummaging ability alone then I would have gone for Iain Milne. The Bear was, without doubt, the hardest scrummager that Scotland have ever produced. Nobody ever got any change out of Milne. He took some dreadful poundings over the years as opposition forwards, sick of the pressure that he put them under, resorted to their fists. But the Bear just got on with his job. Loe, though, gets the nod, but only just, and on the basis of his work outside the scrum.

My locks are Olivier Roumat of France and Ian Jones of New Zealand. They are both modern-day second-row forwards who can win ball in the lineout, provide the muscle in the scrummage but also get about the park like back-row men. Roumat, at 6ft 6in and 17st 5lb, is the ideal size and weight for an international lock. I'm not convinced that giants of 6ft 10in, like England's Martin Bayfield, are ever going to be mobile enough to fulfil the wide-ranging role that I want to see in this World XV. Jones, at the same height as Roumat but a stone and more lighter, isn't that bulky by international standards but he is a fantastically athletic ball-winner at the lineout and, like Roumat, he gets around the paddock at a fair lick of knots.

I've played against both of them and alongside Roumat for the Barbarians. The Frenchman is just unbelievable in the scope of what he is able to do on a rugby field. He likes nothing more than getting the ball in his hands and running for the line. He never thinks twice about it. Some big forwards take fright when they get the ball in open field and the first thing they want to do is to get rid of it. Not Roumat or Jones. They just pin back their ears and tear off upfield.

Wade Dooley and Paul Ackford came into the reckoning. I've played against them and alongside them with the 1989 Lions but I reckon that Roumat and Jones offer more. My Scottish team-mates Damian Cronin, Chris Gray and Andy Reed are tremendous players and they also deserved consideration but I'm happy to stick with Roumat and Jones.

At number 8 I'm going for Dean Richards of England. He is a genuinely world-class player. He always looks as if he is just lumbering around but the amount of work he gets through is just amazing. He seems to suck the game towards him. He doesn't of course, but his ability to read a game is so superb that he is almost always in the right place at the right time. I don't think that there is anybody quite like him for his ability to work out what is going to happen next. He was outstanding with the Lions and, from a scrum-half's point of view he is a really difficult man to play against. Part of my scrummage game is to put pressure on the opposition number 8 when the ball goes to him. Some players, who aren't natural number 8s, are easy to get to. I have the highest regard for England's Mike Teague. He, too, was fantastic with the British Lions in 1989 but he is a blind-side wing-forward, not a number 8, where England played him in their Grand Slam game against us in 1990.

A lot of so-called number 8s — and this includes a lot of international players — just can't pick up from the scrum and feed the scrum-half properly. It is such a crucial part of the number 8 role that you would think that it would be second nature but it isn't. Some of them just can't do it. You have to be a natural ball player to be able to accomplish it properly. It takes a lot of skill to steady the ball under scrummage pressure, with the opposition scrum-half lurking on the horizon, and then to pick it up, drive and feed your own scrum-half.

The crucial moment in that 1990 game againt England came with a mistake by Mike Teague. He knocked on as he tried to pick up a ball from the base of the scrum. The scrummage put-in then went to us and from that we scored. That's suicide for a number 8 but it happened because Mike wasn't a natural in the position. I knew when he was selected for that game that we would be able to put him under pressure. He never looked comfortable in the position. He was slow and predictable and not suited to the role. One of my strong points has always been putting pressure on the opposition number 8 and Teague was one of the easiest I have played against. This sounds like a very harsh verdict on Mike but it wasn't his fault. The problem lay with selection.

If I had been picking the England side then I would have had him at blind-side wing-forward which was where he was the man of the series with the Lions just a year beforehand. I'm glad, though, that the England selectors got it wrong.

Derek White came close to selection for my World XV but I've decided to go with Richards. Derek, like Richards, is a natural number 8. I've played alongside him a lot for Scotland and he was great but the Englishman just brings that wee bit extra to the side.

At open-side wing-forward I'm going to pick the New Zealander Michael Jones. He was the All Black who said 'Never on a Sunday'. He wouldn't play on the Sabbath because of his religious beliefs and I take my hat off to him for that. But what a player he is. I watched him during the 1991 World Cup and I don't think that I've ever seen such a display of non-stop rugby. He was faster than most wingers and, like the Western Samoan that he is, as strong as an ox.

Finlay Calder has to come into the equation somewhere but he played in a different style to Jones. If we knew that the game was going to be a dog-fight then I wouldn't look beyond Fin. He looked after me more times than I care to remember when the going, and the opposition, got tough. But, for the kind of champagne rugby that we hope this Murrayfield testimonial is going to be, Michael Jones is my man.

At blind-side wing-forward is the Tongan Torpedo, Villiame Ofahenagaue. Willie O has to be just about the most devastating close-range runner that I have ever seen. I'd never heard of him until the 1991 World Cup but he made a huge impression during the tournament, not to mention an impression or two on anybody who had the misfortune to run into him as well.

I've not overlooked John Jeffrey. How could I overlook JJ? But what we're looking for here is a back-row blend. Calder, White and Jeffrey were a superb unit for Scotland but, for a one-off game I'm going for Ofahengaue in the number 6 shirt. Mike Teague was there or thereabouts, too, but I don't think that he ever recaptured the form he showed in Australia during 1989 and so Willie O is my choice.

Now I have to choose the skipper. The candidates are Sole, Hastings or Fitzpatrick. I have to admit that I like a forward captaining the side so both David and Sean are, initially, the front-runners. However, Gav has done so superbly well as captain of both Scotland and the Lions — and particularly so when coming through a really tough time with the Scottish side — that I'm going to go with him. I can't separate David and Sean and so I'm going to cop out and make them joint vice-captains. They can fight it out amongst themselves for who is to lead the pack.

The side will be coached by Ian McGeechan and Jim Telfer. Geech has got a rugby brain second to none. He could dissect the opposition and explain just what he expected of his players in a way that I've never heard any other coach do. Jim Telfer would coach the forwards. He is one of the hardest taskmasters that I've ever come across in world rugby but he is a motivator without parallel and with that line-up of players and with these coaches I reckon that my World XV — as they say down my way — would be 'gey ill tae bate'.

Now for the opposition. It's my book and my game and so I get to choose them too!

The full-back has to be Gala's Peter Dods. He was a very fine player and Scotland's full-back during the 1984 Grand Slam season. He was just unlucky to be around at the same time as Gavin Hastings. Nevertheless, Peter went on the 1989 Lions tour to Australia and he's a cert for my Scotland Select.

On the right wing I would have Keith Robertson of Melrose. Keith was always on his toes. You never really knew what was going to happen next when he had the ball. Keith's selection means that there is no place for my Grand Slam team-mate Tony Stanger of Hawick. Tony has said that he doesn't want to play on the wing any longer but he has scored a lot of tries for Scotland and he was certainly a contender for the right-wing berth. Keith, though, provides that degree of the unexpected which a showcase game like this needs.

From an admittedly limited number of possibilites, the only real candidates for the centre positions would be Lineen, Hastings and Alan Tait of Kelso who went away to rugby league after just eight Scottish caps. He was a fine player and I made my Scottish début in the same side as him but we have no way of knowing how good he would have become. Ian Jardine and Graham Shiel have both played at centre for Scotland in my time but I would have no difficulty in going for the 1990 Grand Slam partnership of Scott Hastings and Sean Lineen.

My choice for left winger is Iwan Tukalo. He, too, was a bit of a slippery customer and just like Robertson always kept the opposition guessing. Derek Stark and Kenny Logan came into the reckoning but, to my mind, neither is yet a patch on Tukalo when he was at the top of his form and so 'Tooks' it is.

Because Craig is alongside me in the World XV we have to find another stand-off. I made my Scotland début with the Anglo Richard Cramb at fly-half and, aside from Chic, the only other guys that I've been paired with at senior representative level have been Graham Shiel and Gregor Townsend. Toonie gets the nod. Gregor is a bit of an enigma. He seems to have been around for ages but he is still only a youngster. I think that the Scottish selectors pushed him into the side too quickly. He had a superb Five Nations championship in 1995, before injury put him out of the World Cup, but he really needed a run of good games. He will mature into a fine player for Scotland but I don't know whether, with his capacity for making silly mistakes, that the crucial position of fly-half is the best berth for him. He's playing really well for Scotland in the centre. Nevertheless, for this game I think he deserves to play at fly-half for Scotland in direct opposition to Chic.

The contenders for scrum-half would have to be Greig Oliver, Andy Nicol, Derrick Patterson or Bryan Redpath. I'm going for 'Basil' Redpath. I've only ever seen Patterson play one game for Scotland and that was in the defeat by South Africa in late 1994. I didn't think that he had too bad a game but he was dropped in favour of Redpath. Since he came into the side Basil has more than proved his worth. He has a very fast service and is a good link man. I'd maybe like to see him take the opposition on a wee bit more but that's not his style and he can certainly get the backs moving. The combination of Redpath and Townsend might be a good one. With Redpath's slick service and Townsend's searing acceleration they might well be made for one another.

Greig was a good scrum-half and he's still doing a great job for Hawick at full-back but I think even in his prime he would have found Basil a bit of a handful. Andy Nicol has been blessed with good and bad luck in his Scotland career. Because of injury and because he was understudying me, he's had just the one international season and, at the risk of sounding like a stuck gramophone record, your first season is always the easiest. I think we would have to see more of Andy before we could decide just how good he really is. Only when he has recovered fully from his bad knee injury will that question be answered. For now, though, Basil gets my vote.

Alan Sharp will be at loosehead prop. The Bristol man has got the right attitude in that he is a rough, tough, no-nonsense player who just gets stuck in. He's no David Sole but, then again, few people are. David Hilton did well when he came into the Scotland side while Sharp was out injured but, tough choice though it would be, I prefer Sharp to him.

At hooker is Kenny Milne. I can't overlook him as he got so close to selection for my World XV. Running Kenny close, though, was Gary Callander. The Kelso player was another of those who would have got a barrow-load of caps had it not been for them being around at the same time as a special kind of player. In Gary's case it was Colin Deans. If it hadn't been for Deans then Gary would have had umpteen caps. He was a good player and good thinker about the game. He was a big strong laddie, just like Kenny, and a big hooker just sets the pack up. For that reason I'm discounting Stirling County's Kevin McKenzie. Kevin is a good player but a good big 'un will always be better than a good little 'un. That's tough on Kevin but that's just the way it is. John Allan doesn't enter the equation because I don't think that he should have got into the Scotland side in the first place. I'm choosing the side so, sorry John, yer oot!

Tight-head prop is tricky. Paul Burnell doesn't really come into the reckoning. Paul is a good scrummager but I'm looking for guys who can do more than scrummage. For this reason, but with great difficulty, I'm not going to pick Iain Milne either. I'm going for Peter Wright. The Boroughmuir player was a revelation for Scotland in the 1995 Five Nations Championship and to a lesser extent in the World Cup. He was into everything. He was popping up at centre, taking and giving passes, tackling Jeremy Guscott and generally getting around the paddock like a man possessed. He's my kind of player and he is the tight-head prop for this Scotland side.

To lock the scrum I'd find it very difficult to look beyond the 1990 pairing of Damian Cronin and Chris Gray. I've considered Andy Reed and Shade Munro and, having been mightily impressed by Stewart Campbell in the 1995 Five Nations, I've considered him too. But I'm going to stick with Damian and Chris. They were proven winners and Del Boy is showing that there's still life in the old dog yet. So it's the old firm of Cronin and Gray in the middle row.

I'm not going to mess about at all with the back row. No contest. It has to be Jeffrey, White, Calder. When I was picking my World XV the criteria used was on individual merit. I was still looking for a blend in the back row and I reckon I have that with Jones, Richards and Ofahengaue. However, if I had been picking a ready-made unit then Fin and Co would have gone straight in. As a threesome they were almost telepathic. Each of them seemed to know what the others were doing even without looking. That's the best back row I've ever played with. It will be interesting to see what it's like playing against them!

So, that's it. Roll up, roll up and take your places for the Gary Armstrong testimonial match. It's a pity it'll never take place. I reckon it would have been one hell of a game.

THE WORLD XV

Gavin Hastings (Scotland)
Ieuan Evans (Wales)
Jeremy Guscott (England)
Philippe Sella (France)
David Campese (Australia)
Craig Chalmers (Scotland)
Gary Armstrong (Scotland)
David Sole (Scotland)
Sean Fitzpatrick (New Zealand)
Richard Loe (New Zealand)
Olivier Roumat (France)
Ian Jones (New Zealand)
Willie Ofahengaue (Australia)
Dean Richards (England)
Michael Jones (New Zealand)

SCOTLAND SELECT

Peter Dods (Gala)
Keith Robertson (Melrose)
Sean Lineen (Boroughmuir)
Scott Hastings (Watsonians)
Iwan Tukalo (Selkirk)
Gregor Townsend (Gala)
Bryan Redpath (Melrose)
Alan Sharp (Bristol)
Ken Milne (Heriot's FP)
Peter Wright (Boroughmuir)
Chris Gray (Nottingham)
Damian Cronin (Bourges)
John Jeffrey (Kelso)
Derek White (London Scottish)
Finlay Calder (Stewart's Melville FP)

CHAPTER 11

COUCH POTATO FIGHTS BACK

South Africa (and Nearer Home) 1995

THROUGHOUT the late spring and early summer of 1995 the Murrayfield powers-that-be were sending out subtle hints and signals designed to whet my appetite for the World Cup in South Africa. I was flattered but was still recovering from the knee injury which had kept me out of the game for over a season and, with the exception of some light running and some medically prescribed weights sessions, I hadn't done any serious fitness work since the previous autumn when my preparations for the seven-a-side circuit had been so abruptly curtailed by that training accident at Riverside Park.

As the Scottish selectors finalised their plans for the World Cup squad there were quite a number of players recovering from injury and it was decided to make use of the excellent rehabilitation facilities at the Lilleshall Sports Injury Centre in Shropshire.

My old Jed mentor Roy Laidlaw, in his capacity as National Squad co-ordinator, was placed in charge of the walking wounded and I was asked if I wanted to be included in the party along with Damian Cronin, Andy Reed, Andy Nicol, Alan Sharp and Peter Walton. It was nice to be asked. It's good to know that although you might have been out of sight you weren't out of the

157

selectors' minds. But I was happy with the progress I was making under the guidance of my physiotherapist at the Princess Margaret Rose Hospital in Edinburgh and the last thing I wanted was to rush the healing process. I wanted to get it right and to make sure that, once the start of the new season came along, I would be giving myself the best possible chance of getting back to my previous form and — all else being equal — winning back my Scotland place.

However, as the summer progressed and the World Cup unfolded in all its drama on television, there were times when I wondered whether I had made the right decision.

Even 5,000 miles away, and even from the sometimes distorted view that you get from television, it was obvious to me that Rugby World Cup 1995 was something special. This was big-time rugby both on and off the field. Sitting there in my front room watching Scotland and all the others on the box I just wanted to be there. That was when it was really driven home to me just how much I miss not being involved at international level. I was right not to have been tempted into an early return via the efforts of Lilleshall but I knew the moment I saw Scotland run out to the pitch at Rustenburg to play Ivory Coast in their first game of the tournament that I had been right, too, in my decision to give it one more chance and — fingers crossed — retire from the international arena on my own terms and not be forced into retirement because of injury.

Bryan Redpath, the Melrose scrum-half, is now in the driving seat and he played some great rugby in South Africa. I thought, too, that Derrick Patterson looked good against Tonga. They are completely different players. 'Basil' has that whiplash service of his while Patterson is much more physical and both are going to be hard to dislodge. When you add Andy Nicol to the equation then I know that it is not going to be easy to get back that Scotland number 9 shirt. However, I'm going to give it my best shot and if I don't succeed then I will have satisfied myself that at least I gave it a go.

Scotland played really well in South Africa and here I must take my hat off to Gavin Hastings. After the game against South Africa at the end of 1994 I was one of those who thought that Gavin should have called it a day. But he proved us all wrong. He led by example throughout the Five Nations tournament and in South Africa and it was just a pity that Scotland could not have gone further than they did just to have given Gavin the send-off that he deserved.

The games that really mattered for Scotland were against France and New Zealand. We could and should have beaten France and if we had done that then we wouldn't have played New Zealand in the quarter-finals. But at least against the All Blacks Scotland took the game to them. They didn't just roll over like England did.

Every time I saw the New Zealanders' 19-stone winger Jonah Lomu I was praying that he wouldn't desert to Rugby League. Scotland tour New Zealand in the summer of 1996 and I would love to be there if for no other reason than to have a crack at Lomu. Everybody says that he's invincible and impossible to tackle but there hasn't been a player born who can't be brought down so long as you're brave enough and your technique is sound. Away back at the 1991 World Cup they said the same thing about Vaiga Tuigamala but when we played the All Blacks in Cardiff in the third-place play-off we showed that Inga the Winga wasn't the Superman that the media had made him out to be.

I was champing at the bit while watching the World Cup on television. I've got my hunger back with a vengeance. It's amazing what a year and more on the sidelines can do. Both mentally and physically I'm in better shape than I have been for ages. Those dark days when I turned my back on Scotland and, really, just couldn't be bothered with rugby now seem like an age away. It will be a huge challenge for me to get back to the top and part of that challenge is the readiness to accept that you might fail, very publicly, but I think that I wouldn't be doing myself justice if I didn't at least make the effort. Even if I don't make it then I think that Scottish rugby will have benefited. Competition for places is what makes great teams. If Bryan and Derrick and Andy all know that I'm fighting to win back my place then that will make them try all the harder and, although at the end of the day only one of us will succeed, the international side will have reaped the benefits of our not-so-private little battle.

Just as the first World Cup in 1987 acted as a catalyst for off-field developments in the game then it is clear to me, even from a distance, that the 1995 World Cup will have been one of the great watersheds of the game. The announcement that Rupert Murdoch's media empire was to pump £370 million into the game Down Under with an exclusive contract to televise matches in South Africa, Australia and New Zealand means that the Southern Hemisphere game is now awash with money in a way that it never has been before. Even before Murdoch turned up with his pot of gold the Southern Hemisphere nations were leading the way when it came to looking after their players and I believe that by the time the next World Cup comes around in 1999 then the top players will be paid. So far as I'm concerned there is no doubt about that at all.

Literally within a few weeks of these words being written, the Scottish Rugby Union announced in one of the most momentous decisions ever made at Murrayfield, that — International Board permitting — they were giving their blessing to a professional game. That was a recognition by the Union of the realities which now face the game. Nevertheless, it was a brave and, I'm sure for many, a difficult decision and one for which they should be warmly applauded.

I have been involved in world-class rugby during a transition period. Players of my era have made peanuts while the game itself has made millions. Maybe if I do get back into the Scottish side then I will reap some of the benefits that international players will be expecting as their right from here on in. That isn't my motivation for wanting back to the top but I would be kidding myself if I said that the prospect of making a wee bit of money as compensation for the time and effort that we all put in wasn't attractive.

As I write, the Scottish domestic game is about to undergo a revolution the likes of which it has never seen before. We've got a new league system and, for the first time, the prospect of a Scottish Cup. Both ventures are to be welcomed and serve further to whet the appetite for my return.

For the entire 1994–95 season I had to stand and watch as Jed-Forest were relegated to the new second division. I can't begin to tell you how frustrating that was. At club level my principal ambition now is to see Jed back in the top flight. In the meantime, the introduction of a Cup competition means that clubs like Jed who find themselves out of the élite, eight-team premier division can still have a crack at the top sides in the Cup. Additionally, and this is why the Border League is still worth its place in the calendar, we can still look forward to top-flight competition against the likes of Hawick, Gala and Melrose despite the fact that they are in premier league division one.

During the summer of 1995 the Scottish Rugby Union was defeated in its efforts to ring-fence the game in Scotland by bringing in legislation which would have made it virtually impossible for overseas players to compete in domestic competitions. The SRU wanted players from abroad to be resident in Scotland for three months before they could become eligible for League and Cup rugby in Scotland. Effectively, this would have ruled out the top players from the Southern Hemisphere who would not have had time to finish their season Down Under and then get across here in time to fulfil the three-month quarantine obligations prior to the start of our season.

I can understand what the SRU were trying to do. They wanted to make sure that home-bred talent had the best opportunity of prospering without competition from overseas stars. However, the clubs vetoed the plan when it came before the SRU annual general meeting. And quite right too. There is already existing legislation which means that clubs are not permitted to play more than two incomers. If a safeguard is required — and maybe it is — then that is more than enough. What the SRU wanted to do was shortsighted in the extreme.

There is no doubt in my mind that the more class players who perform regularly in our domestic game then the better our home-bred players will become. If a local player is good enough then he will get into his local side. Already, clubs have a shopping list of players that they want. If they are weak at prop then they will want to go out and get a prop. If they reckon that the team will be improved by the import of a scrum-half then they will put feelers out for a scrum-half. If the domestic talent is good enough then the club wouldn't even think about finding replacements from elsewhere. The bottom line is that if a local player is good enough then he has nothing to fear from folk coming in from outside.

Additionally, there is absolutely no doubt that playing with class players around you improves your game. Look at Sean Lineen when he came to Scotland from New Zealand and enlisted with Boroughmuir. He was a revelation and there's no doubt that his input raised not only the standard at Meggetland but influenced back-play in Scotland as a whole. We should remember, too, that over the last few years, a large number of young Scottish players have gone to New Zealand, Australia and even South Africa to play during our close season. So far as I'm aware there are no restrictions on how and when they are permitted to play.

We shouldn't forget either that 'stars' are what make any game. In rugby, extra spectators will always turn up to watch an Andy Irvine or a David Campese. As rugby moves towards the twenty-first century with more emphasis on marketing and trying to attract youngsters who, maybe, aren't particularly interested in the game, there's no doubt that if some of the All Blacks or the Springboks that the kids have seen on television during the World Cup came to play club rugby in Scotland then, with the right kind of marketing, the Saturday afternoon 'gate' takings would be increased and the game as a whole would benefit accordingly.

As I write, the game in Scotland — and everywhere else for that matter — is on the threshold of a new era. Professionalism, in all of its many guises, is a certainty. The vast majority of players will continue to play for their sheer love of the game. Meanwhile, at the very top, an élite band of players will play for love and money. Internationalists will be paid and will be contracted to their Unions. In Scotland, there are, maybe, half a dozen clubs who will be able to pay at least some of their players in just the same way that 'amateur' cricket clubs, even in Scotland, have a club professional.

Within a couple of years we will see a European championship funded by television. Currently, there isn't a club side in Scotland that could live with the Baths and the Leicesters, the Toulons and the Agens. But if Scotland's representatives in the championship were to be district sides — which is effectively what these big English and French clubs sides are anyway — then we should be able to give a good account of ourselves.

The advent of a Scottish Cup competition is something which most rugby folk have been clamouring after for years. As I've said, it will allow the clubs not competing in the top division of the league to have something really worth while to aim for and, for individual players across the entire spectrum of Scottish rugby, it will provide an additional showcase for them to catch the eye of district and national selectors.

It seems to me that the game is in better fettle than it has been for years and from a player's point of view there are more opportunities for meaningful, enjoyable contests than there have ever been before. I just wish I was ten years younger. Now would be a great time to be starting out on a rugby career awash with fresh challenges and never-ending opportunities.

CHAPTER 12

THE VITAL LINK

Role of the Scrum-Half

THE ESSENCE of scrum-half play is the simplest thing in the world to describe. The scrum-half acts as a link between the forwards and the backs. Within the realms of that role the scrum-half is faced with three basic offensive options: run, pass or kick. In defence the function of the scrum-half is even more simple to describe. It is the tackle, the whole tackle and nothing but the tackle. But, like so much else in life, nothing is ever that simple. These are just the basic building blocks for what is one of the most crucial positions on the pitch.

I was lucky in that with the mini-rugby section at Jed I was given a sound base on which to build. It's essential that you get the basics right if you are to make anything of yourself in the senior game. Different scrum-halves bring different qualities to the game. Some wearers of the number 9 shirt are out-and-out link men with a rocket pass that gets the ball to the stand-off in the twinkling of an eye and others — and I probably fall into this category — play almost like an extra back-row forward.

One thing that all of the best scrum-halves must have, though, is a big heart. You are up there among the heavy traffic mixing it with the forwards and you have to be ready and willing to take the knocks that will inevitably come your way. You also have to be mentally alert and to have almost a sixth sense for reading the game. Probably that is something that the best scrum-halves are born with. I don't really know how I do it but I just have this feeling for the game and for situations that develop in the course of a match. It's almost as if you've seen the movie and have a pretty clear picture of what is going to happen next.

One lesson that has stuck by me since my earliest days at mini-rugby was the cardinal rule never to hand on bad ball. Even if it means that you are going to take a shoeing from the opposition forwards then you should never, ever hand on a ball to your stand-off if it means that he is going to be in trouble. No hospital passes. That was the lesson taught at Riverside when I was a seven-year-old and ever since then I have always tried to look after my stand-off. Other scrum-halves are different. They'll just pass the ball with little thought of the consequences but that has never been my thing. It's really just a case of how you were brought up to play.

In every match situation I aim to keep the opposition guessing. I'll maybe throw out four or five passes and then make a break. The intention is to keep your opponents on their toes and never let them know what you're going to do next. Once you've tested the waters with a couple of breaks then you should put in a couple of kicks. Mix and match the whole time. Especially at international level the opposition coaches will have tried to work out what kind of game you play in order to close you down. But if you vary it throughout the entire course of the match then there's little chance of them bringing their pre-match containment strategies into play.

A good pass is essential in a scrum-half. I think my pass is adequate. It's not in the Exocet missile mould but it does the trick. I've never been one of those blokes like Richard Hill of England who'll practise 50 passes off each hand every night. When I joined Jed-Forest from Jed-Thistle I did a fair amount of passing practice with Roy Laidlaw. We would line up a few balls in front of the Riverside stand and, using first one hand and then the other, I would flick them off the advertising billboards.

I use a spin pass but not in a conventional sense. I use the same technique that served Roy so well. A lot of scrum-halves spin the ball with their left hand over the top of the ball. That makes the ball spin into the stand-off. But I flick my hands in the opposite direction. I bring my right hand up, spinning the ball away from the stand-off. When I'm passing from right to left my right hand comes over the ball and when I'm passing from left to right I spin the ball by flicking my right hand underneath. It may be a bit slower but I've worked on it to make it faster and, in my opinion, it is a better pass for the stand-off because it spins away from him and forces him to run on to the ball. The spin pass is a relatively recent development in the game. The balls used nowadays, with their all-weather coatings, make it so much easier to work up a spin. With the old leather ball that resembled a bar of soap in the rain it would have been virtually impossible to execute a spin but, now, a good spin pass is a vital element in any scrum-half's armoury.

At a scrummage I would also often use a dive pass. That's the classic scrum-half pass and the one that always appears in old photographs. It's not used nearly so much as it was previously but at a scrummage it's ideal. First and foremost what you should be attempting to do is to deliver the ball to your stand-off as quickly as possible and at the scrummage, often, the best way of doing that is to use the dive pass.

I find that with the amount of protection that your wing-forwards can give you at a scrum there really is no excuse for not delivering good, clean ball to your stand-off. Here, though, the key is feet placement. Before you even lay a hand on the ball as it comes out at the rear of a scrummage you must have your feet in the correct position. If your feet aren't in the correct position then you are giving yourself no chance at all of executing a good pass. Once your feet are into the optimum position then everything else just follows on from there. I get my right boot in behind the ball and spread my legs wide to give myself a good platform for executing the pass. Good feet placement means that you have created a solid platform from which to make the pass and, absolutely essentially, you don't have to make an exaggerated wind-up with your hands and arms before off-loading to the fly-half.

The wind-up is a real killer. When I was younger I had a dreadful wind-up and that meant two or three seconds lost. Two or three seconds in which the opposition could make life difficult for you and make life even more difficult for your stand-off. Even now I find that as the season gets under way I have reverted to a wind-up and I have to make a conscious effort to work on my service.

The scrum-half, obviously, has a special relationship with his stand-off but there has to be an understanding, too, between the scrum-half, his number 8 and his hooker.

It's crucially important at a scrummage when a move is planned that both the scrum-half and the number 8 forward know exactly what's on. The number 8 has to know when you want the ball held in the scrummage and, usually, I will tell him before I put the ball into the scrum whether I want it quickly or whether I want him to hold it at his feet. If the opposition scrum-half, for instance, has me under a bit of pressure then, at a couple of scrums, I'll tell the number 8 that I want a couple of channel one balls. Then, at the next scrum, I'll tell him to hold it in. I'll then run out with the ball still at the number 8's feet, the opposition scrum-half will, invariably, follow me and he'll be caught offside. You have to keep the opposition guessing all the time. If my opposite number is concentrating hard on whatever I'm going to do next then it has the effect of putting him off his own game.

I have no real preference in terms of how the ball should come to me from the scrum. Channel one, to the left of the number 8, is probably the quickest and cleanest, but channel two — between the number 8's legs — or channel three, with the number 8 steering the ball to his right, don't cause me any problems. The only ball which I positively dislike is when the number 8 keeps the ball at his feet during a retreating scrum. That's a nightmare. You have a devil of a job to get the ball out of the scrum and you know that when you do eventually manage to extricate it that you're going to get the opposition jumping all over you.

Channel one ball is by far the best for getting the game started again. No doubt some of my team-mates at the coalface will kill me for this but, to my mind, a scrummage is just a means of restarting the game. The quicker the ball is in and out again then the better for the game and for the spectators. Rugby League, to my mind, has got the answer here. You don't have all those heaving scrummages. The ball is just whipped in and out and the game is up and running again.

The other close relationship at a scrummage exists between the hooker and the scrum-half. It's important that you get the put-in right because if you don't then you're just going to be penalised off the park. Early in every game I test out the referee. I'll see how much leeway he's going to give me in terms of the put-in. You'll know soon enough how much he is going to let you away with so far as putting the ball in squint is concerned. After the first couple of put-ins which, maybe, weren't straight down the middle of the tunnel the ref will say to you that you're putting the ball in squint and that if you do it again then he'll penalise you. You take your marker from that.

There's usually a lot going on around the scrummages that most spectators won't know about. As I've said elsewhere I received my introduction to the real world at the hands of the Frenchman Pierre Berbizier during my first visit to Parc des Princes. He was all over me. He stood on my toes, pulled my jersey and tried to punch the ball into the scrum on my put-in when the ref wasn't looking. I have to admit that I've taken a lot of Berbizier's tricks and put them to good use for Scotland and Jed. In fact with Scotland we made a few improvements of our own to the Berbizier bag of tricks.

When David Sole was captain we used to work a trick whereby David, on the left of the front row, would collapse a scrum on the opposition put-in. The ref would toddle off around to the other side of the scrummage to see what was going on and while he was otherwise engaged I would knock the ball out of the opposition scrum-half's hands and into the tunnel for our tight-head prop or hooker to take one, apparently, against the head. Yes, I know it's cheating but, especially at international level, everybody is at it and it's very much a case of 'when in Rome . . .'

Another trick which you have to watch out for is the opposition tight-head taking the ball out of your hands as you're getting ready to put the ball into the scrummage. That's why I never stand too close to the tunnel, just in case the opposition prop reckons that he'll indulge in a wee bit of skulduggery.

At lineouts I tend to stand at the front and work my way back. I much prefer clean, tapped ball that I can ship directly to the stand-off. I'm not a great fan of lineout ball which is taken and driven on. That, in my opinion, just slows the game down. Quickly tapped ball, so long as it is done properly, is in my opinion, the most productive ball and if the ball is tapped badly then it is the scrum-half's job to tidy it up.

Probably the number of injuries that I have suffered in my career, particularly in the last couple of years or so, have come about because of my distaste for shovelling out bad ball. I reckon that it's my job to take the stick rather than passing the problems down the line to the stand-off and those outside him.

Another failing of many young scrum-halves is that before they come to a decision as to what they're going to do with the ball — run, kick or pass — they have a wee look at the opposition. Again this can cost valuable time and this is where the sixth sense that I talk about comes into play. I'm rarely conscious these days of taking a look. I can just sense what's on and what's not on. You have to be totally aware, mentally alert and, all the time, watching not just what's happening in front of you but, out of the corner of your eye, constantly checking where the opposition defence is and whether they're lying flat or deep and where the gaps are.

Particularly, it's part of your duties to tie in the opposition back row. I can still remember a Calcutta Cup game at Murrayfield. It was a lineout on our 22. I was in the process of making a dive pass to Craig Chalmers and, whether I saw him out of the corner of my eye or just sensed that he was there, I reckoned that Mickey Skinner — certainly offside — was bearing down on Chic. I stopped the pass, literally, in mid-air because if I'd gone through with it then the ball and Skinner would have reached Chic at just the same time. Really, it's just like going to work. It's all new to you when you first start but once you've learned the ropes it comes almost as second nature. When you've been playing in the same position, as I have almost constantly, for over 20 years then things just come naturally to you. When Craig and I were playing together for the first time with the South District Union side Roy gave us some advice which I've never forgotten. He said that I had to make sure to hit Craig with my passes every time and he told Craig that when he was kicking for touch then he had to make sure that the ball went out. Distance was secondary, the main thing was to make sure that the ball was kicked dead.

Craig and I seemed to hit if off right from the start when we were teenagers in that SDU side. Many scrum-halves have problems finding their fly-halves the first few times they play together but Craig and I just had a superb understanding right from the start. I like a stand-off who shouts at you all the time and Craig certainly does that. If he's constantly shouting out to you then even if you haven't actually seen where your stand-off is standing then you can pass the ball in the direction of the voice! A stand-off has to be dominant and maybe even a wee bit cocky. He is the man who really runs the show. He calls the backs' moves and he is very much in charge. Chic does all that as to the manner born.

With Scotland Chic and I had a system of codes for right and left. If he wanted the ball going right then he would shout Yes, Yes, Yes. If he shouted No then you knew that he was moving left. At Murrayfield we also used the codes Big Stand and Wee Stand. Big Stand was the West Stand and Wee Stand was the East Stand. If we were playing towards the Haymarket Station end and Craig shouted Wee Stand then I knew that he was moving left, and vice versa. He might shout Short Ball Yes and I would know that he wanted a pop pass to the right. At lineouts if he put his hands on his hips then I knew that he didn't want a ball to run on to. He wanted it straight back because he was kicking.

In a defensive situation it is really down to how hard each individual scrum-half wants to work. If the opposition are running the ball at us then I always get out behind the stand-off and the inside centre, tracking along behind the centres to the corner flag. If someone comes down through the middle then I can be a second line of defence and if the ball goes out wider then the backs will probably be using a drift defence so I let them drift out and I take up position at the corner flag. For a high ball I like to be back either in front of the full-back or behind him, helping the wingers. It really depends how fit you are and how much you want to put yourself about. Some scrum-halves are really lazy in defence and they don't see it as their job to get back to the corner flag or to get back and help with high balls but that's just the way that I have always played and it's never let me down.

The third important element in the scrum-half's repertoire is the kick. Ideally you should be able to kick equally well off either foot. I favour my right foot. I can kick off the left but I've never chanced it in an international. I suppose that could be looked upon as a weakness but it's never caused me any problems yet.

I do a lot of kicking from scrummages and especially from defence. The way I look at it is that if the ball is in the air then there's not a lot that the opposition can do about it and if the kick is a good one then you can turn defence into attack in just a couple of seconds. Usually, when it's in the air it's a 50–50 ball. Scotland have scored a lot of points over the years from cruelly positioned kicks which we have then retrieved. The ideal is to put up the ball which is high enough to let the chasers get underneath it and for it to fall just outside the opposition 22 so that it can't be marked. You want your centres on to the catcher as quick as possible. They must put him to the ground and he has to release. If he does then we should win possession and if he doesn't then we get the penalty.

If I'm playing in a side with a strong lineout I'll often make use of the corner kick. There's nothing better for a forward as he lifts his head from a scrum to see that the scrum-half has taken play 40 metres upfield with a well-placed touch-kick. The touchline kick up the tram-lines is another tactic which often pays handsome dividends. It gives your winger a chance and if the opposition wing or full-back makes a clean catch then there's not a lot he can do with the ball because he's stuck on the touchline with your chasers closing him down.

On a sodden pitch the grubber kick from a scrum is always worth a go. Anything can happen. Devilish little kicks like those put pressure on the full-back. He might knock-on and you've won yourself a scrum in an attacking position. The main thing is to keep the opposition guessing all the time. Your game must never become stereotyped and the opposition should be worrying about you all the time. I would say to any youngster who is just setting out that if you want to be involved on an almost constant basis then scrum-half is the position for you. Unlike the wing, for instance, where you might wait 80 minutes for a couple of passes, at scrum-half you have the ball in your hands every couple of minutes. It's a position where you will undoubtedly receive more than your fair share of knocks but if total involvement is what you are after then scrum-half is the position for you.

CHAPTER 13

LAUGH, I THOUGHT I'D CRY

The Lighter Side

IT WAS the look on the faces of my team-mates which gave the game away. They just stared down at their boots and tried their best not to burst into gales of laughter.

The venue was Mansfield Park, Hawick, in November 1993, and after my self-imposed sabbatical from the scrum-half berth I had been asked to turn out in the number 9 shirt for a Scottish District Select to take on the mighty New Zealand provincial side Auckland. They made me captain and I was taking my responsibilities very seriously indeed. John Rutherford, the Selkirk, Scotland and British Lions stand-off was coaching the side and on the morning of the match he had really laid it on the line.

'This is serious rugby. At this level you've got to make the opposition think that you're a band of raving psychopaths. You've got to make them think that you're a bunch of absolutely ruthless tossers,' said John.

When we got to the ground and were in the dressing-room just before the kick-off I was giving the troops the last-minute call-to-arms. 'And remember,' I told them, 'just as Rudd has said. We've all got to go out there and play like a bunch of tossers.'

As soon as I'd said it I realised that it wasn't quite right. Rutherford, who was standing over in a corner just turned to the wall and one or two of the players let out a stifled giggle. Nobody mentioned my bloomer but afterwards — by which time we'd achieved a notable victory — the boys gave me absolute pelters.

As a gaffe it doesn't come close to that of the former Jed-Forest skipper Jimmy Raeburn who delivered the following peach when the going was getting tough at Riverside: 'Right Jed. This is where the men get sorted out from the boys. Come on boys!' But that kind of humour, unintentional though ours was, is what, for me, makes rugby the game that it is.

The 'crack' is one of the things that most attracts me to the game. I don't know of another sport where you can be knocking seven bells out of each other for 80 minutes and then, when the final whistle sounds, it is all forgotten and you go and have a couple of pints with the enemy in the bar. That is one aspect of the game which I hope will never change even under a more professional set-up.

During the 1993 Five Nations season I was made vice-captain to Gavin Hastings. I was told that if anything happened to Gav then I was to take over as skipper. It was a great honour and I was as chuffed as hell but my great fear was that Gavin would be 'cairted' and I would have to make the speech at the after-match dinner. Gav used to kid me along saying that he would retire 'hurt' a couple of minutes from the end and I would have to make the speech which I so much dreaded.

It was during that season, too, that the wind seemed to blow constantly and Gavin would enlist me to hold the ball for him at goal-kicks. Gav would be teeing up the shot and I would say to him: 'Looks like a nine iron to me' or, even if the kick was away out on the touchline, I would say 'Piece of cake, Gav'. Hastings, exasperated, would eventually say: 'For f . . .'s sake, shut up Gary'. Once, he got his own back on me. I was lying flat on the ground with my finger holding the ball steady in the breeze, Gavin gave it an almighty swipe and almost kicked my finger off. 'Bloody hell, Gav,' I said. 'Sorry, Gary,' he replied and we both looked up and there was the ball soaring between the posts.

The first time that I went to Paris with the Scotland side in 1989 there wasn't much to laugh about on the pitch. We were beaten 19–3 and, as I recount elsewhere, Pierre Berbizier handed me a lesson in the black arts of international scrum-half play. But once the game was over there were laughs aplenty. Damian Cronin, myself and a couple of the boys went to a bar after the official dinner. When we arrived we realised that it was a bar that the French team used and so we decided to make for the Scots' bar in Paris. We hailed a taxi and were speeding through the French capital. It was an estate car and in the back was the driver's shopping. He seemed to have a bag full of fruit. In the dark it looked to me like plums and so I grabbed a handful. I bit into one only to find that they were eggs. I was coughing and spluttering and Damian reckoned that they were turtle's eggs. My hands and face were covered in a black, gooey mess. As soon as we got out of the taxi I broke a couple over Cronin's head. We went off to the toilet in the bar to get cleaned up and a water fight ensued.

By the time we came back out to join the rest of the company — resplendent in their evening dress kilts — we were 'drookit' and covered from head to foot in black turtle egg gunge. It was childish but it was a hoot and just a means of releasing the tensions that build up on international weekends.

Two years later we were back in Paris and, again, there was an incident straight from Fred Karno's circus. Serge Blanco, the darling of French rugby, won his eighty-second cap that afternoon to become the world's most capped player. He also became involved in a ridiculous punch-up with me.

Our coaches, Jim Telfer and Ian McGeechan had told us before the game that we had to be a lot more streetwise than we had been the last time we had been at Parc des Princes. That new-found street wisdom saw me battling Blanco. He had put up a high kick and was chasing after it. Gavin was waiting to make a catch and, with my hands in the air trying to look invisible to the referee, I ran across Blanco's path, ushering him towards the touchline. He was furious. He grabbed my jersey and wouldn't let go. By this time we were rolling about on the ground and the ball was 60 yards away. He still wouldn't let me go and so I whacked him. Still, he had me by the scruff of the neck and so I whacked him again. He went off with a cut face and the French crowd was howling for my blood but I thought nothing more about it. Until later that is.

In Paris one of the customary highlights is the bus-ride from the team hotel to the venue for the post-match banquet. It sounds pretty straightforward, doesn't it? But unless you've experienced it you have no idea what a roller-coaster ride it can be. The bus is escorted by crazy French motorcycle cops who whisk you through central Paris at the most appalling speeds. Another part of the tradition is that while we are waiting to leave the hotel the cops give the Scottish players 'backies' on the BMW motor-bikes. They zoom up and down the street like a bunch of crazed Hell's Angels.

This night, I was sitting with a bottle of beer on the back of a motor-bike when three old ladies walked past on the pavement. They saw me and shouted 'Zer is ze man who hit Blanco' — or something like that — and, waving their umbrellas in the air they charged straight for me. The cop saw what was happening and whisked me off behind the bus. If he hadn't then the old wifies would have to laid into me with their brollies.

An international weekend is a high pressure situation for the players and any little prank which releases the tension can often do a lot of good. During the 1991 World Cup at the Dalmahoy Country Club and Hotel I can recall 'shooting' Gavin with a high-powered water pistol. Craig Chalmers and I had been out buying presents for my youngsters and I bought one of those high-pressure pistols. I was walking around outside and there, through his open bedroom window I saw Gavin fast asleep. I took careful aim. Bull's-eye. And then I scarpered. He suspected me but he never did find out who had soaked him.

The demon drink has led to the downfall of many a player. As you get older you learn how to handle all the booze that can come your way after an international match but one incident which I vividly recall involved a very young Craig Chalmers.

It was one of our first meetings with Ireland and at the post-match banquet Chic fell foul of that awful man Willie Anderson. Craig was seated next to the former Ireland lock and all night long he plied young Chalmers with drink. By the time we came to sing *Auld Lang Syne* Craig was well the worse for wear. What made it worse was that Jim Telfer was sitting at the same table. When we all stood up to join hands for the traditional *Auld Lang Syne*, Craig reckoned he would go one better and hop up on the table. Sadly, the table gave way and Chic ended up, literally and metaphorically, under the table. If looks could have killed then Chic would have been dead meat. Jim Telfer just looked down at him and shook his head in dismay. Craig was put to bed and Willie Anderson had the self-satisfied look of an Irishman who had drunk a Scotsman right under the table. However, as you get older you get wiser and you know to pace yourself.

There has always been a geat spirit within any Scottish side that I have been involved with. You meet up for training sessions throughout the season and by the time the Five Nations tournament comes around you are just like one big happy family. It's that spirit which has often carried Scotland through against technically or physically superior opposition. That, and the 'crack' which is so much part and parcel of the game.

CAREER STATISTICS

Until End of Season 1994–95

SCOTLAND

Tour details and 1991 World Cup appear separately

1988–89	F	A
Australia, Murrayfield	13	32
Wales, Murrayfield*	23	7
England, Twickenham	12	12
Ireland, Murrayfield	37	21
France, Paris	3	19

1989–90		
Fiji, Murrayfield	38	17
Romania, Murrayfield	32	0
Ireland, Dublin	13	10
France, Murrayfield	21	0
Wales, Cardiff	13	9
England, Murrayfield	13	7
New Zealand, Dunedin	16	31
New Zealand, Auckland†	18	21

1990–91

Argentina, Murrayfield*	49	3
France, Paris	9	15
Wales, Murrayfield*	32	12
England, Twickenham	12	21
Ireland, Murrayfield	28	25
Romania, Bucharest	12	18

1992–93

Ireland, Murrayfield	15	3
France, Paris	3	14
Wales, Murrayfield	20	0
England, Twickenham	12	26

1993–94

England, Murrayfield	14	15
Ireland, Dublin	6	6

* Denotes try
† Denotes replaced by Greig Oliver

SCOTLAND 'B'

1987–88	F	A
Italy, Aberdeen*	37	0
France, Chalon-sur-Saône	18	12

* Denotes hat-trick of tries

Represented Scotland at Under-18 youth level (once) and Under-21 level (six times)

Club: Jed Thistle; Jed-Forest (debut 1984)

South of Scotland: Sixteen appearances

Barbarians: Two appearances (v Newport and v New Zealand)

Led Scottish District Select to victory over Auckland at Mansfield Park, Hawick, in November 1993.

Represented Scotland in Australia Bi-centennial seven-a-side tournament, 1988.

THE 1989 BRITISH LIONS IN AUSTRALIA

Full-backs: P.W. Dods (Gala), A.G. Hastings (London Scottish).

Threequarters: J.A. Devereux (Bridgend), J.C. Evans (Llanelli), J.C. Guscott (Bath), M.R. Hall (Cambridge University and Bridgend), S. Hastings (Watsonians), B.J. Mullin (London Irish), C. Oti (Wasps), R. Underwood (Leicester and RAF).

Half-backs: C.R. Andrews* (Wasps), G. Armstrong (Jed-Forest), C.M. Chalmers (Melrose), A. Clement* (Swansea), P.M. Dean (St Mary's College), R.N. Jones (Swansea).

Forwards: P.J. Ackford (Harlequins), F. Calder, captain (Stewart's-Melville FP), G.P. Chilcott (Bath), W.A. Dooley (Preston Grasshoppers), M. Griffiths (Bridgend), J. Jeffrey (Kelso), D.G. Lenihan (Cork Constitution), B.C. Moore (Nottingham), R.L. Norster (Cardiff), D. Richards (Leicester), R.A. Robinson (Bath), S.J. Smith (Ballymena), D.M.B. Sole (Edinburgh Academicals), M.C. Teague (Gloucester), D.B. White (London Scottish), D. Young (Cardiff).

*Replacements.

Manager: D.C.T. Rowlands (Wales).

Coaches: I.R. McGeechan (Scotland) and R.M. Uttley (England).

Medical staff: Dr B. Gilfeather and K. Murphy (both RFU).

Tour record: Played 12   Won 11   Lost 1   Drawn 0

	F	A
Western Australia	44	0
Australia 'B'*	23	18
Queensland	19	15
Queensland 'B'*	30	6
New South Wales	23	21
New South Wales 'B'*	39	19
First Test	12	30
ACT*	41	25
Second Test	19	12
Third Test	19	18
NSW Country XV*	72	13
Anzacs	19	15

*Denotes games played in

SCOTLAND TOUR PARTY IN NEW ZEALAND, 1990

Full-backs: P.W. Dods (Gala), A.G. Hastings (London Scottish).

Threequarters: A. Moore (Edinburgh Academicals), S.T.G. Porter (Malone), A.G. Stanger (Hawick), I. Tukalo (Selkirk), S. Hastings (Watsonians), S.R.P. Lineen (Boroughmuir), A.C. Redpath (Melrose), A.G. Shiel (Melrose).

Half-backs: C.M. Chalmers (Melrose), D.S. Wyllie (Stewart's-Melville FP), G. Armstrong (Jed-Forest), G.H. Oliver (Hawick).

Forwards: A.K. Brewster (Stewart's-Melville FP), A.P. Burnell (London Scottish), I.G. Milne (Heriot's FP), D.M.B. Sole (Edinburgh Academicals), captain, J. Allan (Edinburgh Academicals), K.S. Milne (Heriot's FP), D.F. Cronin (Bath), C.A. Gray (Nottingham), J.F. Richardson (Edinburgh Academicals), G.W. Weir (Melrose), G.A.E. Buchanan-Smith (Heriot's FP), F. Calder (Stewart's-Melville FP), J. Jeffrey (Kelso), D.J. Turnbull (Hawick), G.R. Marshall (Selkirk), D.B. White (London Scottish).

Manager: D.S. Paterson.

Coaches: I.R. McGeechan and D. Grant.

Tour Record: Played 8   Won 5   Lost 2   Drawn 1

	F	A
Poverty Bay–East Coast	45	0
Wellington*	16	16
Nelson Bays-Marlborough	23	6
Canterbury*	21	12
Southland	45	12
First Test*	16	31
Manawatu	19	4
Second Test*†	18	21

*Denotes games played in
†Replaced by Greig Oliver

WORLD CUP 1991

Full-backs: A.G. Hastings (Watsonians), P.W. Dods (Gala).

Threequarters: A.G. Stanger (Hawick), I. Tukalo (Selkirk), S.R.P. Lineen (Boroughmuir), M. Moncrieff (Gala), A.G. Shiel (Melrose), S. Hastings (Watsonians).

Half-backs: C.M. Chalmers (Melrose), D.S. Wyllie (Stewart's-Melville FP), G. Armstrong (Jed-Forest), G.H. Oliver (Hawick).

Forwards: D.M.B. Sole (Edinburgh Academicals), captain, A.P. Burnell (London Scottish), A.G.J. Watt (Glasgow High-Kelvinside), D.F. Milne (Heriot's FP), K.S. Milne (Heriot's FP), J. Allan (Edinburgh Academicals), D.F. Cronin (Bath), G.W. Weir (Melrose), C.A. Gray (Nottingham), F. Calder (Stewart's-Melville FP), J. Jeffrey (Kelso), D.J. Turnbull (Hawick), G.R. Marshall (Selkirk), D.B. White (London Scottish).

Manager: D.S. Paterson.

Coaches: I.R. McGeechan, J.W. Telfer, D. Grant, D.W. Morgan.

Medical staff: Dr Donald Macleod, Dr J.P. Robson, Mr David McLean.

Pool two winners. Quarter-final winners against Western Samoa. Defeated in semi-final against England. Defeated in third-place play-off against New Zealand.

Pool matches:

	F	A
Japan, Murrayfield*	47	9
Zimbabwe, Murrayfield	51	12
Ireland, Murrayfield*†	24	15

Quarter-final:
    Western Samoa, Murrayfield*   28   6

Semi-final:
    England, Murrayfield*   6   9

Third-place play-off:
    New Zealand, Cardiff*   6   13

*Denotes played in
†Denotes try